SECULAR INSTITUTES IN THE CODE OF CANON LAW

A New Vocation in the Church

SECULAR INSTITUTES IN THE CODE OF CANON LAW

A New Vocation in the Church

Edited by
B. M. Ottinger
A. S. Fischer
U.S. Conference of Secular Institutes
1988
Revised 2008

©1988 by the U.S. Conference
of Secular Institutes

Revised 2008

ISBN: 978-0-87061-161-2
Library of Congress Catalog Card Number:88-072379

Printed in the USA

Table of Contents

Preface

It is a privilege for me to write a preface to a book that has been so greatly valued because of the dedication of those who authored this work twenty years ago. In the words of St. Augustine this is a book which is "ever ancient ever new" in telling the story of consecrated secularity as it is addressed in the 1983 Code of Canon Law.

Discovering consecrated life in a secular institute by people in this new millennium has energized the reprinting of this book. For many, both clerics and lay people alike, the living of consecrated life other than in a religious institute is still a foreign concept. Hopefully the reading of this book will provide valuable insight for those discerning such a vocation and it will also continue to be a great resource for those of us who live out the evangelical counsels in a secular institute today.

At the IV World Congress of Secular Institutes Pope John Paul II said:

"You are qualified representatives of an ecclesial reality that has been, especially in this century, the sign of a special 'motion' of the Holy Spirit within the Church of God. The Secular Institutes, in fact, have highlighted the value of consecration even for those who are working 'in the world'; that is, for those who are engaged in worldly activities, both as secular priests and, above all, as lay people. For the laity, in fact, the history of the Secular Institutes marks an important stage in the development of the doctrine regarding the special nature of the lay apostolate, and in the recognition of the universal vocation of the faithful to holiness and the service of Christ. Your mission today has a perspective consolidated by theological tradition: this consists in the 'consecratio mundi,' the consecrated life in the world—that is, by working from within, to lead back to Christ, as the sole head, all earthly realities."

Let us pray that the Lord of the harvest will send laborers into his vineyard.

Fr. George F. Hazler, I.V. Dei
President
USCSI

April 7, 2008

Foreword

With the promulgation of *Provida Mater Ecclesia* in 1947, the Church recognized the validity of the Secular Institute vocation. In revising the 1917 Code of Canon Law, it was necessary to change the section previously entitled "Religious" to that of "Institutes of Consecrated Life" to include this new vocation. Since the promulgation of the 1983 Code, presentations of a historical, theological, and juridical nature have been made to members of Secular Institutes and to priests assisting these Institutes, at local and international conferences, to deepen their knowledge and understanding of the Canons.

This book brings together four of these presentations and two on the history of Secular Institutes to provide a reference and resource document for vocation directors, spiritual directors, seminarians, instructors, and the laity in general, as well as for members of SIs themselves. We recognize some overlapping in these articles as they were given to different groups, however, we feel it is justified in view of the general lack of knowledge of this vocation. Secular Institutes for priests are not being presented in this volume as this important topic deserves its own presentation.

We are grateful to our contributors for allowing us to reprint their presentations and take this opportunity to thank: Professor O. Montevecchi, retired professor of the Sacred Heart University, Milan, Italy; Sr. Sharon Holland, I.H.M., member of the Canon Law Society of America and of the National Conference of Vicars for Religious; Don Mario Albertini, subsecretary of the Sacred Congregation for Religious and Secular Institutes. Our special thanks to Sr. Sharon Holland for reviewing the manuscript and to Fr. Edward Pfnausch, Executive Director of the Canon Law Society of America, for permission to reprint Canons 710–730.

The Editors

CHAPTER I
A General History of Secular Institutes

B.M. Ottinger*

Introduction

Twenty centuries after the coming of Jesus Christ and the establishment of His Church, sacred virginity and perfect chastity consecrated to the service of God continue to flower in the world.

These faithful, consecrated to God through the practice of the evangelical counsels of poverty, chastity, and obedience, are a hymn of praise and glory to the Lord because they represent a triumph of spirit over matter and of grace over nature.

Beginning with the first Fathers of the Church through the Doctors, teachers and ascetics of every century, there has been an unceasing chorus of voices to praise the beauty, merit, and nobility of the consecrated state of life. And the Church, with solicitous care and maternal affection, has always encouraged, sustained, and wisely ordered the way of life for those called to the "state of perfection." Today, following Vatican II, one

---

*Author of Chapters 1 and 2; first president of U.S. Conference of Secular Institutes.

1

speaks rather of "consecration through profession of the evangelical counsels."

The form which this state has taken down through the centuries has differed from time to time, and so has answered the needs of the specific period. For example, most briefly,

- In the first centuries of Christianity men and women, virgins, radiated the light of Christ in the midst of their pagan world; often they paid with their blood for their lives of fidelity.
- During the years when the Roman Empire was declining, hermits lived solitary, penitential lives and so hastened the coming of the Kingdom.
- In the period of the barbarians, the monks saved human civilization with work and prayer in the silence of their monasteries.
- During the Renaissance, the two great mendicant Orders of Franciscans and Dominicans brought the spirit of the Gospel to the ordinary man in the marketplace.
- Following the Protestant Reformation, and the French and Industrial Revolutions, the socially active congregations of men and women appeared with the mission to alleviate the misery and suffering which these revolutions brought and to prepare with education and training the laity who were to reap the benefits of the Industrial Revolution and the formation of towns and factories.
- Today the Lord has issued another call to the laity of the modern world inviting them to dedicate their lives to Him through the same total consecration so as to bring the world back to Christ, while living in the world as consecrated seculars—members of Secular Institutes.

Historical Perspective and Characteristics

In the historical life of the Church, Secular Institutes are relatively new. Attempts to establish associations of persons consecrated to God while living in the world, within their own families and environments, were made centuries ago. First of all was that of Saint Angela Merici in the sixteenth century. But at that time there were insurmountable difficulties depending upon the mentality and social structures: women did not have complete juridical independence, full personal responsibility, and autonomy. And these are necessary if one is to live in the world as a consecrated secular. Consequently, following the death of Saint Angela Merici, the Company of St. Ursula, which she had founded, was guided toward a conventual form of life. But this tiny seed was not dead, only dormant for three and one half centuries. In 1866, as the Company of St. Ursula it regained its intended physiognomy, and today it is a recognized Secular Institute.

With the Decree *Ecclesia Catholica* confirmed on August 11, 1889 by Pope Leo XIII, the first steps of a true and proper association of laity consecrated to God were taken. This Decree gave norms for the approval of organisms whose members remain in the world and do not wear a habit. These organisms were approved as pious associations and the vows of the members were not recognized by the Church nor taken before a superior. Each member took vows privately and each association was under the jurisdiction of a bishop. This was a tiny step forward toward approval and recognition of Secular Institutes by the Church.

The "Why" of Secular Institutes

Years of experimentation preceded the official appearance of the organisms which we today know as Secular Institutes. Influenced very much by life under the almost atheistic dictators of the late nineteenth and early twentieth centuries with their rise in materialistic tendencies, it became increasingly difficult for consecrated men and women to function fully and well in the cause of Christianity. A more subtle, less visible approach was needed, but one, nevertheless, which expressed fully the spirit of total donation of self to God. The European countries were pioneers in this approach to evangelization, and we see in these early groups the foundation for the Secular Institute movement of today.

The war, with its suffering and miseries, its aftermath with the loss of freedom for many people, substantiated the worth of totally consecrated, unknown lay persons in the modern world.

It is true that the task of building a better world, of inserting Christian values within modern structures belongs to all the laity, but especially does it belong to the consecrated secular, who must assume the responsibility of expressing consecration of life in the realities of everyday life. Through complete dedication of self, the consecrated secular offers all to Christ unconditionally so that He may, through their love and sacrifice, reach all persons in every walk of life.

As defined in the 1983 Code, "A secular institute is an institute of consecrated life in which the Christian faithful living in the world strive for the perfection of charity and work for the sanctification of the world especially from within" (c. 710). This definition clearly outlines the charism of Secular Institutes: consecration to God, secularity, apostolate. Many institutes practice "reserve" in regard to the names of their members, not for the purpose of creating an atmosphere of secrecy, but to assure these members freedom of action in their familial, professional, and apostolic environments. Thus they avoid all that might distinguish them from other lay persons and make them appear as quasi-religious without habits.

Today Secular Institutes fall into two categories: institutes of penetration in secular fields, on the frontiers of secular life, and institutes of collaboration in the works of the apostolate.

Father Agostino Gemelli, OFM, priest-founder of the Missionaries of the Kingship of Christ, became acquainted with the fledgling groups of laity in and through his travels for the

University of the Sacred Heart in Milan, Italy. In 1938 he called together representatives of these groups in San Gaul, Switzerland, and their discussions formed a basis for future documents and pronouncements.

With the promulgation of *Provida Mater* in 1947, growth has been noteworthy in both numbers and geographical distribution. Recent statistics show approximately 80,000 lay persons and secular clergy have accepted the call to this vocation in 148 Secular Institutes with formal canonical structure, 52 of which enjoy pontifical approval, extending to almost every country of the world. Particularly impressive is growth behind the Iron and Bamboo curtains. Numerically, institutes for women rank first, those for secular clergy second, and for lay men, third. This is an indication that their existence is not merely accidental but is a work of the Spirit. (*Dialogue*, JAN/MAR 1987)

Papal Documents Governing Secular Institutes

1. *Provida Mater Ecclesia,* the Apostolic Constitution, was issued on February 2, 1947 by Pope Pius XII. This document gave official life within the Church to the groups of totally consecrated laity and secular clergy which it called "Secular Institutes."

It consists of two parts, the historical and doctrinal. It traces and justifies the coming of Secular Institutes against a background of the other official states of perfection to be acquired. It also includes a legal statement of ten articles, *Lex Peculiaris,* which set forth the general pattern which each institute must follow in drawing up its own Constitution and according to which each institute must live.

It opens with a general notion of what a Secular Institute ought to be; presents a definition of these organisms, defines their membership and lays down in general the purpose of such an institute. It placed these groups under the Sacred Congregation of Religious.

This was a new and daring form of consecration. Never before had the Church recognized a life of total consecration without the "safeguard" of community life, public vows, and public witness.

The most important aspects of this document seem to be its breath of vision which allows for the great plurality of present day institutions, and the fact that it opened the way for such institutes by giving them official standing in the Church. To this day it remains a significant document for individual institutes.

2. *Primo Feliciter*

On March 12, 1948, Pope Pius XII again spoke out for the cause of Secular Institutes with this *Motu Proprio.* His main intent seemed to have been his desire to express his approbation and praise for these institutes. He expressed clearly the hope he had for them: "The Holy Spirit . . . has called a multitude of our sons and daughters . . . to the ranks of the Secular Institutes, to make of them in this nonsensical shadow-world to which they do not belong but in which by God's wise ordering they must live, a salt, . . . a light, . . . and a little yeast, . . . to permeate each and all by word, example and in every way, until it forms and shapes the whole of it, making of it a new [leaven] in Christ."

After defining anew these institutes, he dwelt on the secular character which he said constitutes their whole reason for being. Yet he also pointed out the balance that must exist between consecration and secularity if the institutes are to achieve their goal. This is a new emphasis not found in the previous document which leaned much more heavily on the religious character. Here the emphasis shifted to the secular.

3. *Cum Sanctissimus*

Within a month, on March 19, 1948, the Sacred Congregation of Religious issued this instruction of eleven articles regulating in some detail the actual procedure of those who wish to form a Secular Institute in order to obtain approval from the Holy See. Essentially, it remains in effect today.

Importance of these Basic Documents

These three documents can be called the "Magna Carta" of Secular Institutes. They express the thought of the Holy See on Secular Institutes and, while they are few in number, they are broad in scope and leave room for growth. They show clearly that the hierarchy has not entirely created these institutes, it has discerned and approved what was good within the movement born within the Christian people.

The Second Vatican Council

The decrees *Lumen Gentium, Gaudium et spes,* and *Apostolicum actuositatem* refer directly and obliquely to the relationship of the Church and the world and the role of the laity in effecting this relationship.

It is, however, only in *Perfectae caritatis,* the decree on the renewal of religious life, that one finds specific reference to Secular Institutes. Paragraph 11 clearly states that "secular institutes are not religious institutes . . . [but] they involve a true and full profession of the evangelical counsels in the world, recognized by the Church. . . . The institutes themselves ought to preserve their own special character—their secular character, that is to say, to the end that they may be able to carry on effectively and everywhere the apostolate in the world, and, as it were, from the world, for which they were founded."

Papal Messages

It is important to remember that these papal messages follow Vatican II and reflect its thinking.

Pope Paul VI addressed Secular Institutes, their members and directors, on five different occasions. Briefly we have summarized here these messages:

1. *To the Directors General on the occasion of the First World Congress of Secular Institutes on September 26, 1970,* he concentrated on the psychological and spiritual aspect of dedication in Secular Institutes, which he developed in and through the reflective act of conscience and the subsequent free choice which has permitted members to remain secular. He then spoke of the challenges of the vocation lived in the world, of the two kinds of work in which members must be engaged—personal sanctification and consecration of the world. He concluded by giving them three things to remember:

    a. your consecration will not be only a commitment, but it will also be a help, a support, a beatitude to which you can have recourse;

    b. you are in the world, and not of the world, but you are for the world;

    c. you belong to the Church by the special title of consecrated seculars.

2. On the twenty-fifth anniversary of *Provida Mater Ecclesia,* February 2, 1972, Paul VI spoke out quite clearly in sympathy and approval of these Institutes. His Holiness emphasized that the Secular Institutes must be set in the perspective in which Vatican II presented the Church, as a living, visible, and, at the same time, spiritual reality. Members of Secular Institutes share in the faith, the life, the mission, the responsibility of the Church, and yet are distinguished by a gift, a particular charism, of the life-bringing Spirit, given not only for one's personal benefit, but also for the benefit of the whole community. The anniversary of *Provida Mater Ecclesia* was an invitation to Secular

Institutes to check their faithfulness to their original charism characteristic of each.

The audience was reminded that the soul of every Secular Institute member has a deep concern for synthesis, a longing for the simultaneous affirmation of two characteristics: 1) full consecration of life according to the evangelical counsels, and 2) full responsibility for a transforming presence and action within the world, in order to mold it, perfect it and sanctify it. In this framework, the deep and providential coincidences between the charism of Secular Institutes and what was one of the clearest and most important lines of the Council, "the presence of the Church in the world," is clearly seen.

Pope Paul stressed that the dual reality of the nature of members of Secular Institutes was especially geared to assist in narrowing the gap between technical and scientific progress and the growth of faith in the living God. In leading a consecrated life, members of Secular Institutes are the expression of undivided loyalty to Christ and to the Church and through the help of divine grace, they carry out the work of redemption and transformation in the world. Also, the secular character of these consecrated seculars, which is not just a sociological condition, but an attitude, bestows on them the responsibility to be present in the world, to serve it so as to shape it, according to God, in a more just and human order, and thereby to sanctify it from within.

In closing, Pope Paul expressed the desire and hope that Secular Institutes may more and more be models and examples of the spirit which the Council wished to infuse into the Church, in order to overcome the devastating threat of secularism in the world today.

3. On September 20, 1972, Pope Paul VI again addressed the Directors General of Secular Institutes at the organizational meeting of the World Conference in Nemi, Italy. One detects in his message a joyful note when he said that in the future historians will write that this was the period when this new as-

pect of the Christian vocation came into being! He emphasized that "Secular Institutes are at a mysterious confluence between two powerful streams of Christian life" and that "we welcome riches from both," and he referred here to consecration and secularity, both of which he stated are equally essential. And he defined "secularity" as "your specific place of Christian responsibility." Most importantly, he called Secular Institutes an "advanced wing of the Church in the world" and referred to their task in relation to that expressed by the Council documents.

4. On August 25, 1976, the Holy Father again addressed the Directors General and spoke to them of Secular Institutes as a living presence in the service of the Church and of the world. Most particularly, he stressed fidelity—to their mission in the world and to the prayer which must guide and stimulate them. Quite clearly he charged the Institutes with the responsibility of forming their members to live in faithfulness.

5. On February 2, 1977, Pope Paul VI commemorated the thirtieth anniversary of the promulgation of *Provida Mater Ecclesia* by saying that thirty years ago "The Church recognized a new form of consecrated life . . . different from that of religious life not only in its implementation of 'the following of Christ' but also in its way of assuming the Church-world relationship, which is also essential to any Christian vocation."

Pope John Paul II has twice addressed Directors General at their World Congresses:

1. On August 28, 1980, he spoke in the light of modern day evangelization and presented three conditions of fundamental importance if the mission of Secular Institutes is to be effective:

a. "you must be disciples of Christ,
b. you must be competent in your professional field,
c. you must change the world from within."

2. Four years later, August 28, 1984, in keeping with the theme of the Congress, he emphasized the importance of formation modeled on the teachings of Jesus. He then reiterated and amplified his thinking on the three points presented in his 1980 address.

Plenary Assembly of the Sacred Congregation for Religious and Secular Institutes

This Plenary Assembly, held in Rome May 3–5, 1983, examined the identity of Secular Institutes, their history, theological foundation, and their juridical figure. At the conclusion of their sessions, they issued an "Informative Document" which was sent to all national Episcopal Conferences.

In his address at the conclusion of the Assembly, Pope John Paul II recommended that the pastors of the Church "foster among the faithful an understanding, which would not be approximate or generic, but exact, and respectful of the qualifying characteristics of Secular Institutes."

World Conference of Secular Institutes

In 1970 the higher officials of approved Secular Institutes—both of diocesan and pontifical right—met in Rome to form the World Conference of Secular Institutes. Two years later, with the completion of their Statutes, the CMIS was formally established. Since that date it has promoted world congresses every four years and publishes a quarterly journal, *Dialogue,* translated into six languages, and the Acts of the congresses as well as other publications pertinent to the vocation.

The Revised Code of Canon Law

On January 25, 1983, Pope John Paul II decreed the publication of the revised Code of Canon Law. For the first time in the history of the Church, there are 20 canons (710–730) devoted to Secular Institutes in Book II, Title III, Part III (See Appendix B).

Canon 6.1.4 and Part III, Title III: Secular Institutes, abrogate and replace the legal norms of the papal documents *Provida Mater* and *Primo Feliciter.*

CHAPTER II
History of Secular Institutes in the United States

Several years passed before the Apostolic Constitution *Provida Mater Ecclesia,* promulgated in 1947, was translated into English and published in a canon law journal in the USA. Meanwhile, the Spirit was stirring on this side of the Atlantic Ocean and groups of laity interested in lives of total dedication were meeting together to discuss common interests.

While Secular Institutes grew slowly in this country, an organization of Secular Institutes had its ups and downs. Almost exclusively the Institutes in the USA are transplants from Europe. Some American groups neither grew nor sought Secular Institute status. Today there is an indigenous group of men—the Institute of Pius X—with its roots in Manchester, NH but with its largest membership in Canada.

Preliminary Organization: The Center of Information

In 1949 following the translation of *Provida Mater Ecclesia,* a small group of clergy and laity came together to learn more about the lifestyle of consecrated lay persons in the world. The relationship of these persons to the already existing organizations of Catholic Action (well established in Chicago and Washington, D.C.) was of prime interest. Father Joseph Haley, C.S.C., then living at the Holy Cross Monastery on the Catholic University campus, was its prime mover. Many of those interested were Catholic University students.

With the permission of Archbishop Patrick O'Boyle of Washington, D.C., a meeting was held in that city in July 1950, attended by more than 50 persons. The discussion, speculative and practical, resulted in the choosing of Father Haley, now at Notre Dame University, to direct a Center of Information on the life of total dedication in the world and the forms in which it existed in the United States. He was to be assisted by a committee-at-large from various parts of the country.

During the next seven years, congresses were held in various areas of the country—west, southwest, midwest, and east—resulting in the formation of regional committees to extend the services of the Center. Both the committee-at-large and the regional committees felt the need of a more stable organization to assure continuance and development of the Center's aims: to create and maintain a service center of information on the Life of Total Dedication in the World, to coordinate knowledge of dedicated life in the world, and to promote collaboration among societies of dedicated life. The Center sponsored a total of eight Congresses.

In the period 1950–1957, the Center published *Proceedings* of the 1950 and 1952 Congresses, up-to-date directories of the Secular Institutes, pious unions, and aspiring groups in the U.S., various booklets and pamphlets, and the book *Apostolic Sanctity in the World,* a compliation of selected papers presented at the various meetings held during the years 1952–1956.

Realizing the need for understanding and assistance on the part of priests, the Center held a priests' conference in Chicago in 1954, and a committee of priests was organized to further this aspect of the work. A year later, also in Chicago, there was a meeting of 100 persons representing 13 groups in the U.S.

The Conference of the Life of Total Dedication in the World

Delegates from the four U.S. regions met at Notre Dame University 6–7 August 1957 to discuss: 1) the desirability of establishing such a conference; 2) correction of the proposed Statutes; 3) election of a provisional Executive Board. The aims of this Conference were: continuation and expansion of its educational services; assistance and moral support to various dedicated groups, especially new ones; and the fostering of a spirit of cooperation among the groups of persons leading a life of total dedication in the world. Pro-tem officers were:

President and Executive Secretary—Fr. Stephen Hartdegen, OFM
Vice President   —Fr. Roy Patterson
Treasurer   —Barbara Ottinger
Editor of Publications   —Fr. Albert Nimeth, OFM

From the very beginning, this interested group of persons worked with and within the Church, obtaining permission from the Ordinary before holding a Congress, establishing contact with the Sacred Congregation of Religious in 1952, and submitting to that same Congregation the program and speakers for each Congress. The Center had also presented to the Congregation the idea of a more stable organization, but on October 29, 1956, Fr. Larraona (later Cardinal) of the Sacred Congregation wrote to Fr. Haley: "This Sacred Congregation would prefer that the definitive organization of your group, which would be effected by the approval of the Constitutions, await the formation of the Conference of Major Superiors of Men in the United States, which should materialize in the course of the year 1957, and that the group be set up then to function under the direction of this Conference."

Between March and August 1957, regional committees met to draft a proposed constitution prepared by the committee-at-large to form a stable and permanent society to be called "The Conference of the Life of Total Dedication in the World" (CLTDW).

The Conference of Major Superiors of Men approved, on September 29, 1959, the Conference of the Life of Total Dedication in the World, thus opening the way to unlimited possibilities of service to Secular Institutes and their allied associations. At this time there were 28 societies of total dedication in the U.S. Of these, 11 were approved Secular Institutes, 6 were pious associations, 7 were societies not canonically established, and 4, while adhering to total or partial dedication of life to God for the apostolate in the world, did not aspire to become Secular Institutes. Early members and supporters of the CLTDW were: the Company of St. Paul, Missionaries of the Kingship of Christ, Opus Dei (which is now a personal prelature), the Society of the Heart of Jesus, Teresians, Caritas Christi, Our Lady of the Way, Schoenstatt Sisters, and the Oblate Missionaries of Mary Immaculate.

After this recognition by the CMSM, the Conference resumed holding congresses every three years. However, the broad nature of the Conference was of concern to the Sacred Congregation of Religious, as expressed in their 1962 letter:

> It is because there are some elements involved, especially in the title of the Conference, and also in the as yet not clearly defined concept of the exact nature of Secular Institute, which are at the bottom of it . . . there is, for instance, the fact that Secular Institutes, until they are approved as such by the Sacred Congregation of Religious, exist ordinarily as pious unions or associations, and these are under the jurisdiction of the Sacred Congregation of the Council.

At the Triennial General Meeting held in Chicago, March 31–April 5, 1964, Father Bernard Ransing, C.S.C., representing the Sacred Congregation, carried out most faithfully the orders of his superiors to retrench, regroup the Conference to include *only* approved Secular Institutes. In other words, to effect a complete change in the structure of the Conference. The principal purpose was to bring the "Conference more directly and competely under the authority of the (newly named) Congregation for Religious and Secular Institutes. Until now there has been a question of divided jurisdiction."

All external activity came to a halt. The following year the Congregation, over the signature of its Prefect, Cardinal Antoniutti, took the initiative and invited specific persons representing seven approved Secular Institutes to meet to draw up statutes for the "founding of a Conference of Higher Officials of Secular Institutes in North America, similar to the Conference of Major Superiors of Religious Institutes which exist in most of the countries of the world." Father Patrick Clancy, O.P., Conference President, was chosen by the Congregation to chair this meeting held at Villa Cortona Apostolic Center, Bethesda, Md., May 22, 1965. The Institutes which accepted were: Caritas Christi, Missionaries of the Kingship of Christ (women), Company of St. Paul, Society of Our Lady of the Way, Pius X, and the Oblate Missionaries of Mary Immaculate (representing Canada, which made the meeting "North American.")

Two months later, while the Congregation acknowledged that it had only a few observations to make on the Statutes, "other circumstances changed the plan" and the Conference was told to expect no further directives for the present. The "other circumstances" were described in a letter from Father Ransing: "Although the idea of a conference of Major Superiors for Secular Institutes was originally conceived for the United States, at least as an experiment, a European organization is also under way since about a month and a half ago."

The Conference was asked to return to its original status as a center of information. In 1967, Cardinal Antoniutti granted permission to re-activate the group avoiding the use of the word "conference."

Leaders of the various approved Institutes came together and changed the title to "Association" of Secular Institutes. At one of these small meetings, on February 28, 1969 at Villa Cortona, the leaders petitioned Archbishop Verdelli, Under-Secretary of the Congregation, to permit two representatives to attend the World Conference of Secular Institutes to be held in Rome in September 1970.

When finally organized, this Congress was composed of delegates from Secular Institutes—not from national organizations of SIs, and so the conference petition was not officially recognized. However, the two designated representatives, Father Stephen Hartdegen, OFM, and Andree Emery, SOLW, were there representing their Institutes. This Congress marked the first step in the organization of the World Conference of Secular Institutes (CMIS).

It also gave the signal to reactivate the existing Association of Secular Institutes. At meetings of officials held in 1971 and 1972, statutes were drafted and officers elected. These statutes were approved by the Congregation on April 5, 1976 for a six-year period. In 1982 these Statutes were definitively approved under the title U.S. Conference of Secular Institutes (US-CSI).

USCSI

The USCSI has met annually since its inception in 1972. For a time, regional meetings were introduced to which local vocation directors were invited and attendance was enlarged to include all interested Institute members.

A special brochure was prepared for the Eucharistic Congress in Philadelphia in 1976 and distributed from the USCSI booth there. A brief explanation of Secular Institutes in the USA was prepared and inserted in the Bishops' packets at one of their meetings in the late 1970's. The Vocation Committee continues to update these brochures and pamphlets. The USCSI was represented in 1999 at the Bishops' Synod of America and had delegates and an information booth at the International Vocation Congress in Canada in April 2002.

In the late 1970's the Conference petitioned the National Conference of Catholic Bishops to appoint an episcopal moderator. Bishop George Fulcher served in this capacity until his death in 1983. He was succeeded by Bishop Marino, then Auxiliary Bishop of Washington D.C. Additional moderators have been most Rev. Thomas C. Kelly, O.P., now retired Archbishop of Louisville, Kentucky, and most Rev. Dennis M. Schnurr, Bishop of Duluth, Minnesota. The present moderator is Archbishop Joseph Kurtz of Louisville, Kentucky.

The link with the Conference of Major Superiors of Men (CMSM) has been a vital one since 1986. In that year, then President Father Tutas represented CMSM at the 1986 regional meeting of the USCSI in San Antonio, Texas, and Milwaukee, Wisconsin. The USCSI continues to maintain relationships with the CMSM, the U.S. Conference of Catholic Bishops (USCCB), National Conference of Diocesan Vocation Directors (NCDVD), Leadership Conference of Women Religious (LCWR), National Conference of Vicars for Religious (NCVR) and other major organizations including the Conferences of Secular Institutes in Canada and South America, and the World Conference of Secular Institutes (CMIS) in Rome.

From its earliest days as a Center of Information, the value of public relations has been recognized. The CLTDW wrote letters to ordinaries and diocesan vocation directors, prepared speakers to address seminary and college audiences and published "Channels" an annotated listing of approved institutes and other societies of consecrated laity, a quarterly bulletin and informative articles.

Most member institutes are listed in The *Official Catholic Directory* and in the *Catholic Almanac*. The USCSI prepares and updates brochures listing all member institutes and makes them available to diocesan vocation offices. Information, also, is provided at: www.secularinstitutes.org. USCSI continues to recognize the need for increased understanding of this new vocation in the Church and welcomes all requests for further information. Requests may be submitted to the USCSI website or to P.O. Box 4556, 12th St. N.E., Washington D.C. 20017.

CHAPTER III
The Theological-Juridical Dimension of Secular Institutes in the new Code

by O. Montevecchi

It seems opportune to start by giving consideration to the Church-people of God—a living organism, with an interior dynamism put there by the Spirit who guides it. The Church, living and operating in the world, is in continuous transformation: therefore, her institutions, while remaining firm in her theological foundations which came down from the Gospel, are undergoing an evolution so that they can respond to the problems and situations which are present in these changing times. The Code, insofar as it is a normative text, tries to fix the discipline of the Church in definition, in formulae. It can only limit itself to tracing directive lines because life is so varied, so rich, more complex than can be addressed in a code of laws. By limiting itself only to general directive lines, it leaves a margin of freedom, of movement, of development to the very institutions which fall under its laws. It does not exclude the possibility of inserting others which may arise from time to time. The more restrictive it is, the more quickly is the Code itself overcome by life. This is what happened to the 1917 Code, at least to that part which pertains to the present topic.

In fact, we are dealing with that portion which belongs to the life and holiness of the Church (c. 574); more than ever before this asks for a theological foundation. But in a new way it touches the Church's relationship with the life of the secular city and, therefore, it deals with the manner in which the Church responds to the problems which grow out of this relationship. We are concerned here with the question of Secular Institutes contained in Book II, People of God, Part III, Institutions of Consecrated Life—canons 710-730.

It is noteworthy to realize that this part of the Code has been one of the most discussed and laborious to complete. Not only did they translate into this legislation what was elaborated upon in Vatican Council II, especially in the Constitution *Lumen Gentium* and in the Decree *Perfectae Caritatis*, but it also introduces new approaches which have matured during the years following the Council, and even from the promulgation of the 1917 Code. Some of these existed in germ from the end of the last century—this is especially true in regard to forms of consecration to God.

This entire part is rich in new ideas, not only in the way of presenting the material. In brief:

1) The title "consecrated life," is an expression taken from the Conciliar documents, really from the Decree *Perfectae Caritatis*, where it does not appear in the title which speaks of "the renewal of religious life." But it does in the context which spells out what this state of life consists of and it emphasizes one special aspect: "it has its deep roots in baptismal consecration and is the most perfect expression of it" (PC 5). The term "consecrated life" expresses what the various forms of this life share in common, while "religious life" in its traditional meaning fixed by fifteen centuries of history is not adapted to some of the more recent forms which stem directly from secular life and which remain inserted in it.

2) The link "consecration-mission" visible in all types of institutes, even contemplative ones.

3) The recognition of a "just autonomy" juridically recognized in the different institutes expresses an insistence on the duties which they have to be the faithful custodians of the intentions and plans of the founders, approved by the Church, relative to the nature, end, spirit, and purpose of the Institute, such as its healthy traditions. All this is defined as "the patrimony of the institute" (c. 578). While there is a general expression of the differences to be found in Institutes, the intent is not leveling as was true in the Code of 1917. Then, while working with an organized synthesis of laws for the first time, which the Church through the centuries had emanated for religious institutes, it attempted to unify them. Thus in 1921 in the directive which the Sacred Congregation of Religious gave to the various Orders and Congregations to revise their Constitutions so as to adapt them to the 1917 Code, they were to use as much as possible the same language as was in the Code. It is helpful to know this because one can then better understand the climate and atmosphere of those years when what we now know as Secular Institutes were just emerging.

A healthy newness of this new Code can be found in its simple presentation. This expresses change in the manner of understanding the life and function of institutes of consecrated life in the Church. Thanks to this way of understanding such functions, Secular Institutes have been able to find their place in a section which constitutes an absolutely new approach in the Code. Secular Institutes are dealt with in Title III of this first section (cc. 710–730), but they are preannounced in a specific manner by a very brief sentence worthy of attention found in the General Norms in c. 577:

> In the Church there are many institutes of consecrated life, with gifts that differ according to the graces given them: they more closely follow Christ praying, or Christ proclaiming the Kingdom of God,

or Christ doing good to people, or Christ in dialogue with the people of this world, but always Christ doing the will of the Father.

This affirms that some institutes have the gift of grace, that is, the charism of following Christ in his "sharing the life of man in the world" (in *saeculo*). They follow Christ who has willed to lead the life of a worker "in his day and in his country" (*Gaudium et Spes,* 32). It is the spirit of the Incarnation lived in the fullest, with extreme consequences. It is clear that in saying "spirit of the incarnation" one does not mean to draw a line between incarnation and eschatology (two aspects which coexist in varying degrees in every christian vocation).

The sentence from c. 577 cited above is meaningful and new; even in the Decree *Perfectae Caritatis,* there is nothing similar. It gives its own meaning specifically to the followers of Christ who are members of institutes. It lays an evangelical and theological foundation for their way of realizing it, aligning it with other ways of following Christ which through the centuries has been and is being realized in the Church, but at the same time giving it its own character.

Now we have come to the point of defining a Secular Institute. But to do this and to understand how they have finally achieved their own place in the Code, and, therefore, have their own juridical-theological dimensions, we must briefly look at how they were born and how they have developed.

Historic Background

A form of consecration to God lived in the world, in one's own family, existed in the first three or four centuries of christianity. This was in the form of consecrated virginity and the celibate "for the kingdom," based on integral observation of the Gospel. A precedent from ancient history, but very meaningful. Among the christians isolated and dispersed in a society still largely pagan, this vocation to consecration to God lived in the world flowered as the seed of renewal and the leaven hidden in the mass. Then, in the fourth and fifth centuries, common life in monasteries took shape. Its great development was in Medieval times when consecration in the world practically disappeared until modern times.

Attempts to build associations of persons consecrated to God while living in the world, in their own families and social environments, were made in earlier days—first of all that of St. Angela Merici in the sixteenth century. But at that time, the difficulties were insurmountable, especially where women were concerned. The mentality and social structure were against this. After the death of St. Angela Merici, the Company of St. Ursula, founded by her, was decisively and rapidly moved toward a conventual form by the men who then ruled the Church.

In the last century, the first true attempts were made in the establishment of associations of laity consecrated to God. At this same time also, the first interventions of the Church, precisely with the Decree *Ecclesia Catholica*, were confirmed in 1889 by Pope Leo XIII. This Decree gave norms for the approval of organisms whose members remain in the world and do not wear a habit which distinguishes them from other laity. It stated that they must be established as Pious Associations whose bonds are not recognized by the Church and they are not taken before Superiors, but privately by each member. Juridically each association is placed under its own bishop. It did not speak of consecration but it recognized the existence of pious associations of laity living in the world whose members individually and privately pledge themselves to follow the evangelical counsels.

For some years nothing more was done apparently. But at the beginning of the century in Paris, the group "Notre Dame du Travail" was born. It was founded by Father Eymieu. In Spain there arose the Teresian Institutions and Opus Dei and much later in France, at Marseille, the Union Caritas Christi. These were all movements which had in common the inspiration to be associations of laity consecrated to God in the world for the apostolate.

To understand the reasons which determined the birth of these associations, we must be aware of the events and social and political changes of the second half of the nineteenth century. These were transforming European christianity and creating crises for the institutions and values which had been acceptable up to that time. Atheism was growing in strength through scientific and technical conquests. It presented these as incompatible with faith. A materialistic mentality engulfed a large segment of the people, especially the middle class. History was interpreted only in the light of economic laws and class struggle. Anticlericalism was on the increase; it limited the action of the priest and prevented his access to many environments. All this created a climate in which there was felt the need to witness to one's faith as a lay christian and the urgency of apostolic action as almost the only possibility.

In Italy at the end of the last century and the beginning of this century, there was a strong movement of militant laity in Catholic Action. This influenced greatly the preparation of strong, robust men and women who pledged themselves to work in the religious and social apostolates of the day. Precisely this new bond of the laity along with a more authentic Christian formation breathed into some of them the desire to make a total gift of self. There was a great flowering of priestly and religious vocations, but there were also those who did not wish to leave the world for the convent since they saw in the world a very broad field of apostolate. Here they could dedicate themselves with all their energies by working for the kingdom of God. In this they saw the best way of making a total gift of self for the apostolate. In this they could empower it supernaturally. Then this ideal began to take shape: consecration of self to God while remaining in the world and working within it for the coming of the kingdom of God. What we speak of today as the charism of the Secular Institute—consecration, secularity, apostolate—was already clearly outlined here.

These movements wanted to work within the Church and for the Church; therefore, they desired Church recognition. But there were many serious difficulties. It seemed almost revolutionary to try to reconcile consecration to God with the condition of laity living in the world in a way of life that was not religious, without habit or convent.

The Code of Canon Law prepared during these years and promulgated in 1917 did not give space to hope. In fact, hope was one of its greatest obstacles. In this Code mention was made of the various kinds of lay associations, but the profession of the evangelical counsels and then consecration to God remained the exclusive right of the religious, distinguishing them from the laity and imposing on them common life and detachment from the world. The rigid character of the Code did not give rise to the hope that within it one could reach understanding and recognition as associations of laity consecrated to God. The terms "laity-consecration" seemed mutually exclusive.

In spite of this, during the first ten years of this century, movements of intense vitality multiplied. Given the difficulty expressed above, some of these movements flowered and oriented themselves toward a religious or quasi-religious form of life. Others more faithful to their lay character remained in a precarious position, some supported by the protection of a bishop. Others followed the guidelines of Benedict XV and attached themselves to religious orders (Franciscan, Dominican, others) creating organisms with the characteristics of Third Orders (*sui generis*) with vows but without habits and common life. However, this dependence on religious orders did not soon grant the autonomy which these new organisms needed, considering their apostolic purpose and their need to be fully lay. Pius XI saw this clearly. Toward the end of the year 1924, he advised the founders of some such organizations to abandon their juridical dependence on religous orders and to attach themselves to the Roman Curia, that is, to the Congregation of Religious because it was responsible for consecrated life or as it was then termed "states of perfection."

This Congregation studied the problem for some years but found an insurmountable obstacle in the fact that these men and women wished to remain lay in spite of their will to consecrate their lives to God. Toward the end of 1931, the Congregation of the Council became involved in this question because it was charged with directing all things "lay." But this Congregation did not hide its perplexity caused by the will of these lay people to dedicate their lives to God. While it made suggested modifications to the Rules and Constitutions of these associations, it did not reach a satisfactory solution precisely because it abolished their consecration, at least as a recognized fact.

Meanwhile new movements were appearing everywhere. In May 1938, there was held in St. Gaul, Switzerland a meeting authorized by Pius XI for the founders and directors of twenty such associations of LAITY CONSECRATED TO GOD from the different countries of Europe. Father Gemelli chaired this meeting. This Franciscan had carried forward for almost twenty years the "Pious Society of the Missionaries of the Kingship of Christ," which he had founded with Armida Barelli. This gathering at St. Gaul solidified the basic identity of their aspirations. Together they agreed to ask the Holy See for the recognition of their associations of laity consecrated to God in the world for the apostolate.

After the convention, strengthened by this experience, Father Gemelli and Joseph Dossetti compiled a "Historical-Juridical-Canonical Memoria on Associations of Laity Consecrated to God in the World." It presented the problem of these groups in clear and courageous terms. It was sent to the Holy See in 1939. Pius XI had died in February of that year, and he was succeeded by Pius XII. He received a copy of this "Memoria," as did the Congregation of the Council and the Cardinals. In November came the order from the Congregation of the Holy

Office to retract the Memoria. Father Gemelli obeyed at once. The Constitutions of some Institutes were sent to the Holy Office and returned without comment, or with few observations. This was very significant, because it was not known at what point they appeared new or almost revolutionary or what they proposed. After the intervention of the Holy Office, the situation of lay movements of this kind remained confused and uncertain. For a time it seemed that they had reached a dead end. Returning to the Congregation of the Council was practically going back to the guidelines of the decree *Ecclesia Catholica* of 1889. The slight approval granted by the Congregation, according to these guidelines, the abolishing of the already recognized consecration, left dissatisfaction within the institutes that had received it.

Provida Mater Ecclesia

These institutes now realize that this intermediate period during which the entire problem was looked into resulted in the promulgation of the Apostolic Constitution *Provida Mater Ecclesia* in February 1947. It traced in summary a history of the "states of perfection," from religious orders to congregations to societies of common life. As a last step along this path, there are the new institutes of laity and of secular priests consecrated to God. To them the name Secular Institutes was given. A decisive step, a conquest, which gave a juridical foundation and a place in the Church to this new form of consecrated life. With an innovation which went beyond the Code of Canon Law, secularity and consecration were synthesized into a vital whole.

Today in rereading *Provida Mater*, the effort to enter into a new concept of consecration to God is apparent. The tone is that of one who has seen the authentic type of consecration in religious life. There is a constant reference to this as the single term of comparison. To affirm that consecration in Secular Institutes is full and authentic, they are called "almost religious." The impression of adapting religious life to secular life is even more visible in *Lex peculiaris* which accompanied the Constitution. This explains why, while some associations of consecrated laity immediately sought approval as Secular Institutes, there was confusion in others. Primarily, they asked if the secularity granted would be true and would it be safeguarded by the organisms which would be approved as Secular Institutes by the Sacred Congregation of Religious and upon which they were to depend. Therefore, there were some associations which resisted and asked for time.

On March 12, 1948, Pius XII presented the motu proprio *Primo Feliciter.* It not only clarified *Provida Mater,* but in some points offered the key for its correct interpretation, with a new development. The tone and emphasis of the motu proprio are geared toward secularity, not in the sense that it should be considered more important than consecration, but in the sense that it be considered an essential element, the "reason for being" of Secular Institutes. The social and professional environment, the circumstances and style of secular life are highlighted. While *Provida Mater* adapted the "life of perfection" of religious to secular life, *Primo Feliciter* put the accent on the duty to maintain all that was proper to secular life as long as it was not opposed to consecration. It conceived the apostolate of members of Secular Institutes as that of permeating society by living and working within it in order to be the salt and the leaven which flavors and changes the mass. It did not insist on specific works of the apostolate, but it affirmed that the entire life of the members is to be translated into apostolate.

Secular Consecration

Consecration to God lived in the world was something so new that one could not expect to find immediately in the Constitutions of the various Institutes an exact balanced, harmonious sythesis between consecration and secularity. Above all it was difficult to distinguish that which was essential in consecration and that which is marginal or rooted in other forms of life. This work had to be done by the Institutes themselves. In the meantime at the request of the various Institutes, the Sacred Congregation declared the bonds which members assumed as "social" (vow for chastity and vow or promise for poverty and obedience) since they are made before the superiors in an Institute approved by the Church. It sanctioned the legitimacy of the secret (reserve) in regard to members' names, a norm already in force in some Institutes, especially in those that were very secular.

However, the papal documents did not dispel the confusion, especially on the part of theologians. They kept asking: are members of Secular Institutes authentic laity or are they a half step between laity and religious? Are Secular Institutes a last stronghold of the religious or do they constitute an elevation, through the counsels, of the lay state? There were many discussions on secularity because, notwithstanding the affirmation of the official documents, there seemed to be a problem in harmonizing full secularity with full consecration. This was especially true on the part of the religious and the clergy who tended to identify the lay state with matrimony; and because for over a thousand years, they had identified consecration to God through the counsels with religious life. So we had to face the problem of creating an authentic secular asceticism which did not repeat the models and plans of religious life, but was inspired directly by the Gospel; then it could adapt to the needs of the environmental and existential conditions of those who live in the world.

Vatican II and Paul VI

Then Vatican II came along. The Council has explicitly affirmed some principles in which one finds motivation of the deepest and most valid nature, thus giving credence to the vocation of the laity consecrated to God in the world. In particular: the substantial goodness not only of the world created by God but of that which man has achieved with the gifts God has given him—human progress; the recognition of the dignity and autonomy of the secular city and the duty which each man has to assume in it; their personal responsibility in keeping with the vocation God has given them; the dignity of the laity incorporated in the Body of Christ through baptism and made sharers in the priestly, prophetic, and royal office of Christ; their mission in the world that must express the spirit of Christ and with Christ lead it back to God; the vocation to holiness common to all men regardless of their state in life; a unitarian and grandiose vision of the created universe and of human history which has its foundation and vertex in Christ in whom all creation is summarized, finds its center and is led back to the Father: man's vocation is to be united to Christ and with Him to lead all creation back to the Father. These are the foundation stones of every vocation lived in the world.

However, the Council said very little about Secular Institutes. In the decree *Perfectae Caritatis,* only paragraph 11 is given to Secular Institutes. This seems somewhat of an anomaly inasmuch as in the beginning it declares that Secular Institutes are not religious institutes and yet inserts the topic in a document which concerns religious life and its renewal. In the decree *Ad Gentes* (40), one finds the affirmation that missionary service can be rendered also by consecrated laity in the world. Nothing more! It seemed almost incredulous that in the decree on the *Apostolate of the Laity,* Secular Institutes were not even mentioned. This would almost seem a reason to negate the lay state of members of Secular Institutes. *Lumen Gentium* does not mention secular consecration, although it gives good guidelines on secularity of the laity (31).

From all this has stemmed other discussions on the nature of Secular Institutes and the position of their members, with a tendency to negate full secularity and the authentic lay state. In reality, the question had not yet matured; the time was not yet. Among the Council fathers, there was little knowledge of Secular Institutes. Only paragraph 11 of *Perfectae Caritatis* reassured members of Secular Institutes as to their identity. Notwithstanding the anomaly of paragraph 11, it does contain synthetically all the characteristics of such a consecration. It expresses in concise terms the basic concepts of *Provida Mater Ecclesia* and of *Primo Feliciter,* and it avoids some of the ambiguities present in these documents.

It is worthwhile to recall the International Congress of Secular Institutes held in Rome in 1970, and the important message which Cardinal Antoniutti, Prefect of the Sacred Congregation of Religious, gave on Secular Institutes. Above all he cautioned Secular Institutes not to assume religious forms and that religious institutes should not imitate secular lifestyle because between the two "there is a precise and intrinsic difference." This affirmation was important because it destroyed the concept that the two could be one. This is both absurd and dangerous, contrary to the Spirit which gives rise in the Church to different vocations to build up the Body of Christ.

Through the gradual conquest of firm points and reassurance regarding the nature of Secular Institutes and the life of their members, the discourses of Paul VI took on a unique importance. One hears his echo in some of the canons of the new Code, or better yet, some canons of the new Code would not have been so formulated without the discourses of Paul VI to Secular Institutes. This Pope noted "the profound and providential coincidence between the charism of Secular Institutes and that which has been called one of the most important and clearest guidelines of the Council: the presence of the Church in the world."

In his discourse on September 26, 1970, Paul said that "already before the Council this aspect of consecrated life had been anticipated existentially because today there is greater need of specialized witness, examples, dispositions, and mission of the Church in the world." In 1972, in speaking to members of Secular Institutes, he affirmed that the secularity is rather an attitude, the attitude of people who are aware that they have a responsibility, being in the world, to serve the world, to make it as God would have it, more just, more human, to sanctify it from within. "To be in the world, that is, to be committed to secular values, is your way of being the Church, of making the Church present, of working out your own salvation and being heralds of redemption. The condition in which you live, your life description in human society becomes your theological self and your way of bringing salvation into the realm of reality for all the world. Your existential and sociological condition becomes your theological reality. Therefore you are not consecrated because you remain in the world, not consecrated while not being religious as *Primo Feliciter* and *Perfectae Caritatis* had said, but you are consecrated while remaining in the world."

With this we can measure how far we have gone since the days of *Provida Mater Ecclesia*. After this long premise, we are ready to examine the canons of the new Code which concern Secular Institutes: cc 710–730.

Canons for Secular Institutes

C. 710. This canon expresses the three elements which constitute the "charism" proper to Secular Institutes: secularity, consecration, apostolate. The expression *consecrated life* is much better than "state of perfection" or "consecrated state"; it renders the idea of spiritual dynamism requested of each one who is consecrated to God, but above all, of those who follow this lifestyle. The idea of total involvement of the person and her activities, even in the areas and aspects of life that are considered "profane." Her entire life is given to God: all that she is and does is for Him.

"... The faithful living in the world," —not just because

they live in the world, but, while living in the world: life in the world is the essential and characteristic element of this form of consecration, just as detachment from the world is essential and characteristic of the life of religious (c. 707.3).

". . . strive for perfection of charity and endeavor to contribute to the sanctification of the world." To strive for the perfection of charity is the end of every Christian—love of God above all things and neighbor for love of God. The one who is consecrated to God assumes this duty in a radical manner, giving herself completely to Him and through Him to one's fellowmen without being limited by a family of her own. The duty to sanctify the world is essential for these Institutes as the striving for the perfection of charity: it is their own mission and their reason for being. Therefore, this duty comprises part of the definition of a Secular Institute, equal to the duty of consecration.

". . . especially from within." Without being detached from the world inasmuch as members continue to be inserted in the "earthly city" and to being a living and operative part of it. It is the mission of the secular laity to orientate earthly reality toward God, the mission which members of Secular Institutes assume totally, reinforced by consecration which makes them completely available to God.

C.712. The meaning and value of the three principal evangelical counsels has already been treated in the general norms of the Code, cc. 599–601. Here we want to note that consecration through the evangelical counsels in Secular Institutes is full and complete; there is no question of "being almost as good as."

Two preoccupations come to light in this canon; 1) to safeguard their own proper and original character, the "charism" of each individual Institute as expressed in the Constitution of each Secular Institute, and 2) to safeguard secularity which is characteristic of all these Institutes. On the other hand, the expression "the secular character proper to the institute," admits to a certain pluralism, at least concerning the meaning of secularity. Look back to canons 598–601. It is interesting because these canons already anticipate for all institutes of consecrated life respect for their differences, especially in defining the bonds of the members "taking account of its own special character and purposes." It also directs that "All members . . . direct their lives according to the institute's own law and so strive for the perfection of their state."

These affirmations are very important for Secular Institutes because they authorize them to point out to their members a proper lifestyle, their own way, which rises from the Gospel, of living the evangelical counsels in secular life. In fact, it is a question of finding ways and forms for living them in the world, with the means and forms which secular life offers, in the conditions, circumstances, and occasions, extremely varied, complex and unpredictable but which are always present. This in no way mitigates the austerity or lessens the content of the evangelical counsels themselves adapting them to life in the world. On the contrary, it gives them a full and specific meaning and realizations in such a way that by consecrating themselves to God, members of Secular Institutes assume some duties and bonds which have adequate and real content and are not in imitation of those of religious on a reduced scale. This subject is of the utmost importance for members of Secular Institutes and should be further developed.

C. 713. 1) This canon is inspired directly by the motu proprio *Primo Feliciter* in regard to "leaven." Paul VI in some of his discourses also spoke in like manner: "a presence and a transforming action within the world, to model it, perfect it, sanctify it." Consecration and apostolic duty are not presented as two elements distinct one from the other. Apostolic action is seen as an expression and realization of one's own consecration. It is a very strong characteristic of the vocation of members of Secular Institutes. Here the Code goes beyond the juridical aspects and plunges deeply into trying to define the spirituality of this state of consecrated life.

2) ". . . in the world and from within the world." This expression is first found in the "Memoria" of Father Gemelli (1939). Here he said, "While in religious or quasi-religious associations, the one who enters dedicates himself to promote the coming of the reign of Christ in the world with prayer and action, always working in the world but from outside the world; the one who enters this new form of consecration, consecrates himself to work with the same intensity and totality for the same end, but he works in the world and from within the world." The expression appeared in the motu proprio *Primo Feleciter* in the Latin expression, "*In saeculo . . . ac veluti ex saeculo.*" It appears again in paragraph 11 of *Perfectae Caritatis* and now its juridical dimension is found in the Code "in saeculo et ex saeculo" with the opportune omission of the world "*veluti,*" which seemed to indicate a secularity that was not complete but only almost.

Participation in the evangelizing mission of the Church is exercised by members of Secular Institutes above all "by their witness of a christian life." Christian life within the world is that led in the family, in one's profession or occupation, in social life by sharing the problems and difficulties proper to these environments and by living with a Gospel spirit. In addition, through the witness of "fidelity to one's own consecration." This is the witness of a gospel life lived by observing the counsels: a chaste life, detached from wealth, in a continuous search for adherence to the will of God in every circumstance. It should demonstrate that the Gospel can be lived profoundly in the so-called "profane" circumstances of life.

". . . by the assistance they give in directing temporal affairs to God and in animating the world by the power of the Gospel." This is the direct action of the secular laity in the structure of the earthly city of which they are a part and in which they live. This is according to the principles enunciated in the Constitution *Lumen Gentium* (31) and in several passages of *Gaudium et spes.*

This asks for an explanation of the motives and meaning of

practicing reserve where the names of members are concerned. This reserve along with the absence of any exterior sign is a norm for some institutes. The reason for using reserve where names of members are concerned is to avoid distinguishing or separating members of Secular Institutes from the other laity with whom they live and work. They want to guarantee in their working and living environments the authentic meaning of their actions: they act under their own personal responsibility as do other laity. They want to avoid being thought of as *religious* who act in the name of their institute and according to the directives of their superiors. Obviously those institutes which have their own works and forms of fraternal life under the same roof have no need of reserve. It is also obvious that the reserve concerns family members, professional and social associates, but not ecclesiastical authority (bishops, for example). Religious render witness by distinguishing themselves from the laity even through the wearing of a habit. The consecrated secular renders witness by showing how she lives the Gospel in the ordinary events of life and thus brings the world back to the reign of God.

"... offer their cooperation to serve the ecclesial community in accordance with the secular manner of life proper to them." Please note that this collaboration is not their prime task; and wherever offered it must be accomplished according to the secular lifestyle proper to a Secular Institute. In other words, done as it is done by all other faithful laity.

Paragraph 3 of canon 713 concerns members of priests institutes.

C.714. Members of Secular Institutes live as do other lay persons in their day and country. Many members of Secular Institutes remain living as they were before becoming members as long as they are not in contrast with their consecration. Their existential condition in the world becomes their place and way of bearing witness. They share all the problems of other seculars: work, living conditions, etc.

C.715. This concerns members of priests institutes.

C.716. Active participation in the life of the institute and the pledge of its members to conserve unity among themselves is very important for members of Secular Institutes inasmuch as they do not have common life. What unites them is primarily a spiritual bond, "unity of spirit" or, as is said here, the spirituality of the institute. This should be strongly felt and assimilated by individual members (especially in those institutes whose members have different professions and apostolates). Dispersed in the world, they must feel strongly the bond of fraternity which unites them; they must be faithful to all the prayer exercises, to the study projects, to fraternal meetings, etc.

CC.717 and 718 concern the government of the institutes and the administration of its goods. Note that moderators are reminded of their responsibility to preserve "unity of spirit" and to promote "the active participation of the members." C. 718 expresses the admonition to favor Gospel poverty in the administration of its goods.

C. 719. These paragraphs emphasize the importance of prayer and praise, in all its aspects, particularly in regard to the celebration of the Eucharist. There is nothing explicitly said about devotion to the Madonna. What was said in c. 663.4 could be repeated here: "They are to have a special devotion to the Madonna, to the Virgin Mother of God, the example and protectress of all consecrated life, including by the way, the rosary." Members of Secular Institutes need her protection in a special way. Note also: the freedom of choice and the manner of spiritual direction which, however, is declared necessary. The canon recognizes the possible role of helper and guide in this area even in the *responsibles,* but always the freedom of the individual is recognized.

CC 720-721. These concern admission to the institute. Note number 3 of canon 721: "For a person to be received into the institute, that degree of maturity is required which is necessary to live the life of the institute properly." It is clear that maturity should be evaluated in relation to the obligations, lifestyle and nature of the institute. Secular consecration requires a special maturity, a strong sense of responsibility to be able to assume and to live the evangelical counsels in the world and to give witness to Christ in all the expressions of life without the support and defense of common life and of the presence of superiors. It is not an easy vocation. This is proven by the fact that the Code fixes at 12 months the minimum period of initial formation for religious institutes while prescribing a minimum of two years for Secular Institutes (c. 722). There follows a period of temporary incorporation for not less than five years, before attaining to perpetual and definitive incorporation in the institute (c. 723).

C. 724 deals with permanent formation of both the human and divine sciences. This includes preparation and updating in one's professional field so one can be more competent and better prepared. One must be current in understanding the social, economic and political problems of the day according to the position and condition of the individual members in society and the country in which they live. It is obvious that moderators and/or the institutes themselves cannot directly furnish preparation and updating in specific fields; however, they have the responsibility to direct, advise, orientate members toward the information. All of this is specific and special to members of Secular Institutes. It stems directly from the nature of their vocation and gives them a way of responding adequately to it. Their consecration invests the entire complexity of reality called *profane* and which must also be assumed into the reign of God. In Christ the sacred and profane, the divine and human, join together and are led back to God. United in Christ, the Word Incarnate, members of Secular Institutes are called to collaborate in this work.

CHAPTER IV
The Church's New Code of Canon Law

by Sr. Sharon Holland, I.H.M.

For Secular Institutes members, surely one of the most significant aspects of the new Code of Canon Law is that section which deals explicitly with their institutes. The former code, published in 1917, preceded their official recognition in the Church, through *Provida Mater Ecclesia,* by thirty years. It made no reference to Secular Institutes. Today's code embraces not only the newer form of consecrated life which won the acknowledgement and praise of Pius XII, but throughout, it reflects wide-sweeping changes initiated by Vatican II. Its canons, reduced in number from 2,414 to 1,752, are reordered to follow the lines of conciliar thought.

It was Pope John XXIII who first called for the revision of the Church's law. On the same day, January 25, 1959, he announced his intention for a council of the church. Twenty-four years and three sovereign pontiffs later, the new law was promulated on January 25, 1983. It had been necessary to wait until the Council gave fresh expression to the Church's self-understanding and doctrine. Then the new law was shaped accordingly.

Repeatedly, over the years, Pope Paul VI urged canonists to search deeply in scripture and theology for inspiration and direction. He insisted that they write law to reflect the essence of a Church in which the primary law is love, the gift of the Holy Spirit, given through faith in Christ. It must be a law unique to the Church, and not excessively based on that of any civil society.

Building on the foundation of his predecessor, Pope John Paul II strongly expressed the role of law in the Church, in the Apostolic Constitution with which he promulgated the new law—*Sacrae Disciplinae Leges*. He observed there that the very purpose of the revision was to better adapt law to the saving mission entrusted to the Church by Christ. Continuing, he stated:

> The Code is in no way intended as a substitute for faith, grace, charisms, and especially charity in the life of the Church and of the faithful. On the contrary, its purpose is rather to create such an order in the ecclesial society that, while assigning the primacy to love, grace, and charisms, it at the same time renders their organic development easier in the life of both the ecclesial society and the individual persons who belong to it.

The Church, then, must be characterised by faith and grace and charisms—especially charity. Drawing upon the Council's teachings, the Holy Father highlighted four elements characterizing a true and genuine image of the Church:

1. The Church is a People of God, within which hierarchical authority is understood as service.
2. The Church is a communion, within which there is the inter-relatedness, for example, of the universal Church and the particular Churches and of primacy and collegiality.

3. All members of the Church have their proper sharing in the threefold office of Christ as priest (sanctifying office), prophet (teaching office), and king (governing office). All members also have common rights and obligations.
4. The Church is urgently concerned with ecumenism.

These themes which characterize the Church, must also inform the Church's law. A skeletal outline of the new Code gives an overview of its content and helps situate the parts described below:

   I. General Norms
  II. The People of God
 III. The Teaching Office of the Church
 IV. The Office of Sanctifying in the Church
  V. The Temporal Goods of the Church
 VI. Sanctions in the Church
VII. Processes

In a particular way, Book II of the new Code is its heart and an ebodiment of many of the key concepts cited by the Holy Father. Entitled "The People of God," the book is composed of three parts: 1) The Christian Faithful, 2) the Hierarchical Constitution of the Church, and 3) Institutes of Consecrated Life and Societies of Apostolic Life. The opening canon of the book sets forth the dignity and responsibility which flow from Christian baptism (c. 204).

This whole second book, focusing on the persons and communities which constitute the Church, frequently repeats the mandate all have received to participate in the Church's evangelical mission. The initial canon on the obligations and rights of all combines the mandate with an expression of radical equality among the baptized (c. 208).

The responsibility of all for the spread of the Gospel is a thread weaving throughout the canons. This is particularly evident in the listings of obligations and rights. All have the right and duty to work at spreading the message of salvation so that it reaches all persons in all places (c. 211). All have a right to undertake apostolic initiatives, using the name "Catholic" with ecclesiastical permission (c. 216).

In a very particular way, the role of the laity, by virtue of baptism and confirmation is stressed. The new canons show the relevance of this for Institute members. Canon 711 recognizes that the canonical condition of Secular Institute members within the People of God is not changed: lay persons remain a part of the laity and secular clerics remain a part of the diocesan presbyterate. They are obliged by the common norms for all institutes of consecrated life (c. 573–606) but they do not lose their status as true laity or diocesan priests. Those who are aware of the decades of controversy over whether Institute members truly could be called laity, will realize the significance of these statements. Missionaries of the Kingship of Christ may recall the original intent of Father Agostino Gemelli as reflected in the full title of the *Memoria* "Associations of *Laity* Consecrated to God in the World." (Emphasis added.)

The special role of laypersons is expressed as follows in the Canons:

> . . . to work as individuals or in associations so that the divine message of salvation becomes known and accepted by all persons throughout the world; this obligation has a greater impelling force in those circumstances in which people can hear the gospel and know Christ only through lay persons.

> Each lay person in accord with his or her condition is bound by a special duty to imbue and perfect the order of temporal affairs with the spirit of the gospel; they thus give witness to Christ in a special way in carrying out those affairs and in exercising secular duties (c. 225).

Surely these words resonate in a particular way with members of Secular Institutes who recall, for example, the words of Pius XII in *Primo Feliciter:*

... the proper and special character of these institutes, that is, their *secular* character, which constitute their whole reason for existence, must always stand out clearly in everything (II).

The roles which all have in the Church are further developed in those Books which take their titles from the various dimensions of the threefold mission spoken of above. Book III, the Teaching Mission of the Church, and Book IV, the Sanctifying Mission of the Church, both set forth new expectations for all of the baptized.

There is no separate Book on the governing office of the Church, but the canons on that subject are newly located in the Code's Book I, General Norms. This is significant because it signals a new openness to lay persons holding certain offices in the Church, which once were reserved to clerics.

Canon 228 specifically recognizes this. Throughout the canons there are examples of offices now open to the laity, especially in chanceries and tribunals. Where a shortage of priests creates priestless parishes, lay persons may also be designated to participate in the exercise of pastoral care (c. 517.2).

Expressions of the obligations and rights of all persons in the Church are very broad and do not require appointment to office or the exercise of particular functions within the Church. These canons could offer special challenge and encouragement to members of Secular Institutes, who, observing discretion in their consecration and secularity in lifestyle, are committed to living their baptismal vocation to the full.

All members of the faithful are charged with the obligation of maintaining communion with the Church and carrying out their duties with diligence (c. 209). They are called to obedience toward pastors (c. 212), and obliged to contribute to the support of the Church, promote social justice, and give assistance to the poor (c. 222).

In many cases, even within the same canons, obligations are paralleled by rights. All have a right to Christian education (c.

217) and to freedom of inquiry in the study of sacred sciences (c. 218). Likewise, they have the right to worship in their own rite and to follow their own form of spiritual life, as long as it is consonant with the teaching of the Church (c. 214). The canons also note the right of all to receive assistance from their pastors out of the spiritual goods of the Church, especially the Word and Sacraments (c. 213).

The faithful have the right, not only to make their needs known to their pastors, but also to express their opinions in matters pertaining to the good of the Church (c. 212). Further, all have a right to their good reputation (c. 220) and to a forum in which to vindicate their rights (c. 221).

Obviously there is a necessary interplay between rights and responsibilities. The final canon on obligations and rights requires that all exercise their rights with due regard to the common good, the rights of others and their duties toward others (c. 223).

In canons speaking specifically of the laity, some obligations and rights are further developed or supplemented. The right and duty of all to acquire Christian doctrine, to pursue higher degrees in sacred sciences, and to receive a mandate to teach those disciplines is expressed in c. 229. Canon 230 describes the "lay ministries" which involve liturgical roles. Although *permanent* installation in the ministries of lector and acolyte is limited at this time to lay men, the law does not curtail the present practice of designating both men and women as lectors and extraordinary ministers of the Eucharist for a specific term of service.

Finally, the canons now include the Church's teaching on a just wage, expressing the right of those employed by the Church to decent remuneration which enables them to provide for themselves and their families. The requirements of civil law must be observed and provision made for pensions, social security, and health benefits (c. 231).

The Council's renewed focus on the dignity of all through

baptism, and the consequent role of laity in the mission of the Church, is clearly recognized in the canons. Once again, this may have special meaning for Institute members who seek in a unique way to promote the Kingdom of Christ through their secular consecration. In this context, one is reminded of the words of Father Gemelli in his *Memoria:*

> . . . their professional activity, while remaining formally in the world and of the world, while remaining in appearances, the undifferentiated natural activity of an individual, in reality is profoundly emptied of every finality and earthly and personal affection or interest, and is transformed into a collective and supernatural instrument of Christian conquest.

Whether the Church is spoken of as People of God, communion, or through some other image used by the Council, there remains the primacy of a mission which Christ entrusted to it—the proclamation to all of the Good News, the reconciliation of all, through Christ, to the Father. Pope John Paul II has recognized the law of the Church as an instrument in service to that mission. In an address given February 3, 1983, he again insisted upon the law's fidelity to the newness of the Council and the primacy of the Gospel law of love:

> The legitimate place due in the Church to law is confirmed and justified in the measure in which it conforms to and reflects the new spiritual and pastoral climate: in serving the cause of justice, the law must be always more and better inspired by the law-commandment of charity, being enlivened and vitalized by it.

CHAPTER V
Secular Institutes in the Code

by Sr. Sharon Holland, I.H.M.

When the work of revising the 1917 Code of Canon Law was divided up among the various commissions of canonists, one group was assigned the section entitled "De Religiosis." Before long the group realized that their task could not be achieved under that title. The official recognition of Secular Institutes by Pius XII in 1947 dictated not only a new title for their section but a new structure for the entire law on institutes of consecrated life.

The 1983 Code embodies those realizations in that part of the law entitled "Institutes of Consecrated Life" (cc. 573–730). Situated within Book II, the People of God, these canons regulate the lives of both religious and secular institutes. The first 34 canons (cc. 573–606) apply to both kinds of institutes, expressing both the essential theological foundations of consecration of life, and the basic canonical principles applicable to all institutes of consecrated life. Following the norms common to all institutes are 103 canons on religious institutes (cc. 607–709), and 21 on Secular Institutes (cc. 710–730).

To examine the law's treatment of Secular Institutes, the first and third sets of these canons must be studied. These now replace that section of *Provida Mater Ecclesia* which was the *Lex peculiaris* for Secular Institutes. Once again it should be noted that the entirely new structure—as well as title—is concrete recognition of that which members of Secular Institutes proposed and believed long before *Provida Mater* declared their life a true "state of perfection." Missionares of the Kingship are aware that this was the whole argument of Father Agostino Gemelli in the *Memoria* of 1939.

Canon 573 introduces the law on institutes of consecrated life with a synthetic theological expression. It condenses the theology of *Lumen Gentium* VI, and *Perfectae Caritatis,* carefully avoiding such concepts as public vows and community life which are peculiar to religious. The teaching contained in the canon focuses on the primacy of God, the permanence of commitment, and the evangelical and ecclesial dimensions of the life described. These concepts are further expressed in c. 574, which also stresses that the life is a vocation and gift initiated by God.

In subsequent theological canons, there is expressed the notion of the evangelical counsels as a gift of Christ to the Church (c. 575) over which the Church may and must exercise jurisdiction (c. 576). The diversity of gifts or charisms manifest in institutes of consecrated life is recognized in c. 577. Although the text is essentially based on *Lumen Gentium* 46, the phrase on sharing life with others in the world was added so the canon would more clearly include Secular Institutes.

> In the Church there are very many institutes of consecrated life which have different gifts according to the grace which has been given them: they follow Christ more closely as He prays, announces the Kingdom of God, performs good works for peoples, shares His life with them in the world, and yet always does the will of the Father (c. 577).

The following canon mandates fidelity to the intentions and determinations of founders and foundresses (c. 578). This very important norm is cited in subsequent texts which speak of the autonomy and proper heritage of each institute (c. 586) and in that which designates the major contents of constitutions (c. 587).

A series of canons follow which deal with technical dimensions such as erection, aggregation, division, merger, suppression, and other juridic changes in institutes (cc. 579–585). Canon 587 states the general principles governing the writing of constitutions and other collections of law proper to each institute.

Further technical aspects follow: how institutes are identified as clerical or lay (c. 588); how they are identified as pontifical or diocesan (c. 589); how they relate to various ecclesiastical authorities (cc. 590–595). Canon 596 speaks of the power of "superiors and chapters" as defined in universal law and constitutions. This unusual lapse into typically religious language is perhaps explained by the fact that in an earlier draft this text was combined with article 2 of the canon which specifically addresses clerical, religious institutes.

In the general norms, the canon on admission to institutes of consecrated life is very broad: the individual must be a Catholic of right intention, with the qualities required by law and free of impediments (c. 597). For Secular Institutes, this is supplemented by c. 720 recognizing the role of major moderators with their councils in admitting candidates, and c. 721 listing impediments: one not yet 18 years of age, bound by sacred bonds in another institute of consecrated life, or incorporated into a society, or bound by marriage bonds. Maturity for the life to be lived is a necessary condition; proper law can add conditions or other impediments.

It is necessary for every institute to describe in constitutions, how members are to observe the evangelical counsels, as well as other obligations proper to their state (c. 598). The three canons which follow express the theological and juridical foundations of each of the evangelical counsels. Each canon begins with the gospel inspiration for its practice, and then states the general canonical requirements. The new structure of the law keeps in view the awareness that the counsels of poverty and obedience will be lived out with considerable diversity between religious and secular institute members.

What was stated in c. 598 about constitutions defining the obligations flowing from the counsels is repeated in c. 712, specifically for Secular Institutes. Their constitutions must also specify the kind of sacred bonds to be used for undertaking these obligations. Of particular importance, given what Pius XII called "the proper and special character" of the institutes (*Primo Feliciter*, II), the canon requires that the constitutions must always preserve "in its way of life the distinctive secularity of the institute."

The formulation of the common norms, c. 602, was carefully worded to allow for the diversity between religious and secular institutes:

> The life of brothers or sisters (*vita fraterna*) proper to each institute, by which all members are united together like a special family in Christ, is to be determined in such a way that it becomes a mutual support for all in fulfilling the vocation of each member. Moreover by their communion as brothers or sisters (*fraterna communiona*) rooted in and built on love, the members are to be an example of universal reconciliation in Christ (c. 602).

This *vita fraterna* by which members are bound, studiously avoids the suggestion of the common life or community living of religious. Here the canon refers to such unifying forces as common vocation, charism, and spirituality. In contrast to c. 607, which calls for religious to live this *vita fraterna* "in common," c. 714 addressed to Secular Institutes notes that they lead their life "in the ordinary conditions of the world." This may be alone, with their respective families or in groups (in *vita fraternae coetu*). In the latter, specifically religious language of the common life and all it implies is avoided.

A further description of what this term means for Secular Institutes is found in c. 716. Besides the call to participation in the life of the institute, members of the same institute are urged "to maintain communion among themselves."

Canons Specific to SIs

The section of the law specifically addressed to Secular Institutes opens with a canon which recognizes the unique identity of this vocation. A Secular Institute is an institute of consecrated life in which the Christian faithful living in the world strive for the pefection of charity and work for the sanctification of the world, especially from within (c. 710).

Since the canons recognize that the juridic condition of institute members within the People of God is unchanged (c. 711), it follows that their role within the mission of the Church is that proper to the laity or the diocesan clergy.

Canon 713 uses the characteristic image of leaven in describing institute members as persons who "strive to imbue all things with the spirit of the gospel . . ." Much earlier, *Provida Mater* had spoken of Secular Institutes members as "the leaven of rechristianization for families, professions and civil society . . ." (Introduction). A year later in *Primo Feliciter,* Pius XII had spoken more eloquently of this small but active leaven at work everywhere "until the whole mass is transformed and wholly leavened in Christ" (PF, Intro.). This appeared again in *Perfectae Caritatis,* 11.

If these words are familiar, those of the second article of the canon may be more so.

> Lay members share in the Church's evangelizing task in the world and of the world through their witness of a Christian life and fidelity toward their consecration, and through their efforts to order

temporal things according to God and inform the world by the power of the gospel. Also, they cooperate in serving the ecclesial community, according to their particular secular way of life (c. 713.2).

For years following *Evangelii Nuntiandi* (1975), institute members studied ways of participating in the Church's task of evangelization. A fundamental principle—that the member's entire life must become apostolate (*Primo Feliciter*, II)—is reflected both in this canon and in c. 722 on formation.

The terminology used for members working both in and from within the world again resonates back to the *Memoria* of Gemelli, who envisioned consecrated lay persons working on the world from within (*sul mondo dal di dentro del mondo*). Some years later this understanding was repeated by Pius XII with the Latin expression "non tantum *in saeculo, sed veluti ex saeculo . . .*" (PF, II). This concept next appeared in *Perfectae Caritatis*, n. 11: *apostolatus in saeculo ac veluti ex saeculo.*

While the English translation could lose the clear relationship of this, to past texts, the canons repeatedly underline the necessity of fidelity to the secular character of this vocation. There is an assumption that members are working in the midst of the temporal affairs which they wish to inform with the power of the Gospel—from within. Even their direct service to the ecclesial community must be faithful to their secular way of life.

In service of this mission, the canons outline the basic elements of a sound spiritual life: prayer, Scripture, retreat, the Eucharistic celebration, the Sacrament of Penance and spiritual direction (c. 719).

The importance of on-going formation of members—a continuing area of concern for the institutes—is reiterated in c. 724. The terminology, based on *Perfectae Caritatis*, n. 11, calls for formation in matters both human and divine. Provision for this is a serious responsibility of moderators.

Others of the canons deal with various technical aspects.

Government in Secular Institutes is left largely to constitutions, although there is a stated requirement that the "supreme moderator"—the highest office of authority—must be definitively incorporated (c. 717).

Canon 718 provides that any institute-owned goods are subject to the Code's Book V on temporal goods and requires that each institute's proper law provide a way of supporting those who work for the institute. A final set of canons provide for separation from the institute through transfer or an indult from the competent ecclesiastical authority (cc. 726–730).

Secular Institutes and the Local Church

The fifty-five canons relating to Secular Institutes at last place their long-awaited recognition in the universal law of the Church. Still, they are often little known or understood. It is a sign of the Church's serious interest in this unique vocation that the 1983 plenary session of the Sacred Congregation for Religious and Secular Institutes had as its theme, "The Identity and Mission of Secular Institutes Today." Their concern that these institutes be better known and understood throughout the world led them to mandate an "Informative Document" which was sent to bishops throughout the world.

During the course of the plenaria, Cardinal Pironio, then Prefect of the Sacred Congregation, spoke of the institutes as an "ecclesial fact" and a gift of the Spirit which "precedes any theological understanding or juridical provisions."

At the close of the session, the Holy Father urged a closer rapport between institutes and the local church:

Should there be a development and strengthening of secular institutes the local Churches could not but gain by it. While respecting the specific character of each one, the secular institutes should understand and take on the pastoral needs of the local Churches and encourage their members to live attentively sharing the hopes, fatigues, projects and anxieties, spiritual wealth and limitations, in a word, in communion with the reality of their Church. Secular Institutes as well as the Pastors should make it a subject of deeper study and concern to recognize and call for their contribution according to each one's particular nature (May 5, 1983).

In the same address, Pope John Paul II stressed the responsibility of pastors. It is incumbent upon them, the Holy Father noted, to offer Secular Institutes all of the doctrinal riches of which they have need for the fulfillment of their vocation.

A letter from the members of the *Plenaria* addressed to Secular Institutes recognized, as had Paul VI, that institutes express the presence in the world of the Church, which seeks to be "leaven and soul" of human society. Thus they urge members: "Be jealously faithful to your vocation, grow in holiness, that holiness to which all of the faithful are called and to which you must give privileged testimony."

CHAPTER VI
Secular Institutes and the Code of Canon Law: General Considerations

by Msgr. Mario Albertini

Three General Considerations

1. The first deals with the fact that the Secular Institutes are now in the Code and in a particular position.

The juridical existence of the Secular Institutes are not sanctioned by the 1917 Code, but by an Apostolic Constitution of 1947, *Provida Mater*, and subsequent complementary documents.

Now the Code, "the principle legislative document of the Church" (Apostolic Constitution *Sacrae Disciplinae*) gives them a complete and systematic legislative framework which is also the fruit of the experience garnered down through these years.

The actual position is in Book II, "De Populo Dei," in the section entitled "de institutis vitae consecratae." The first title of 34 canons in this section deal with the norms common to all institutes of consecrated life; the third title has 21 canons specific to Secular Institutes, and the second title contain 103 canons relative to religious institutes.

The significance of this position is the clear affirmation that the Secular Institutes are of consecrated life in the full sense, and are clearly distinct from the religious institutes (cf. below). 2. The second consideration stems from the approach given to the entire Code and in particular to the Book, The People of God: the reference is to the fact that the doctrine of the Council has been assumed as an explicit foundation, source, and criteria for the interpretation of law.

This aspect is distinctly evident in relation to the Secular Institutes insofar as the ecclesiology of Vatican II touches the essential core of their vocation: the Church-world relationship, the clear affirmation of the universal vocation to sanctity, the acknowledgement of the rights and duties of baptized persons.

Pursuant to the application of the magisterium of the Popes to the Secular Institutes, this ecclesiology makes it possible to have a much better vision of the place Secular Institutes have occupied in the Church over the last 37 years and now occupy in the Code.

3. There is also a third and important consideration. The Code will permit and promote the passage of Secular Institutes from a situation in which they were either unknown or ignored to a situation in which they have the right to be known and in which the other ecclesial components have the duty to acknowledge them. This is a consideration which touches upon a painful aspect in the history of Secular Institutes and voices a hope harbored by all Secular Institutes.

Actual Content of the Canons

1. The descriptive definition of these institutes is given in positive terms, stating that they are institutes of consecrated life with the connotation of secularity (c. 710).

These two elements—consecrated life and secularity—are inseparable and are to be studied jointly in order to understand Secular Institutes. With very much the same language do they surface in the successive canons. The result is that, in order to avoid a falsification of the theological nature even more so than the juridical nature of these institutes, it is necessary to adopt a unitary approach.

The "consecrated life" component is defined in the canons to all the institutes mentioned earlier. It cannot be identified with "religious life" as so very often has been done and continues to be done. This achievement makes it possible to speak about Secular Institutes without having to repeat that they pertain to and are of consecrated life and are not religious (cf. *Perfectae Caritatis*, n. 11) without classifying them on a lower level.

The "secularity" component in which "their raison d'etre subsists" (*Primo Feliciter*, II) is presented not only as a de facto situation (*in saeculo*) but also and especially as a mission in order to contribute to the sanctification of the world *praesertim ab intus.*

This component is most especially stressed in relationship to the apostolate (cf. below), but it is also interesting to find it in c. 711 and c. 712.

Canon 711 states that, with due regard for the prescriptions of consecrated life, the laity in Secular Institutes are laity to all intents and purposes, and therefore applicable to them are the canons relative to the rights and duties of the lay faithful. The priests in Secular Institutes are subject to the norms of common law for the secular clergy.

Canon 712 deals with the evangelical counsels and refers the definition of the subsequent obligations to the constitutions of the individual institutes in order that the testimony capacity according to the distinctive secularity be assured in the lifestyle.
2. The apostolate is expressed in precise terms in c. 713.

Provida Mater requested Secular Institutes to exercise the apostolate in full. *Primo Feliciter* added that "the entire life must be converted into apostolate . . . '*in saeculo, sed veluti ex* saeculo'. . . ." *Perfectae Caritatis* reiterates that Secular Institutes emerged for an apostolate "*in saeculo ac veluti ex saeculo.*"

Canon 713.2 embodies the formula, leaving out the *veluti* and thereby reinforcing it. And then it specifies: through the witness of a Christian life given totally to God and to one's brethren, and in the effort to order temporal things according to God and inform the world by the power of the gospel. This final expression is taken almost word for word from *Lumen Gentium* n. 31, dedicated to the laity, and *Apostolicum Actuositatem* 2, and is also an echo of *Evangelii Nuntiandi* 70. Therefore, the apostolate of Secular Institutes is identified with the apostolate to which the laity, insofar as laity with their specialization of presence in the world and a presence reflecting the assumption of values which exist in the world, are called to order all of reality to God.

This apostolate which is characteristic of laity therefore becomes a specific vocation for the members of Secular Institutes: they consecrate themselves to God precisely in order to live this commitment in a fuller way.

The same paragraph adds that these institutes can also render a service in the ecclesial community, but as lay persons with the specific characteristic of their secular way of life. This terminology as well is taken from *Apostolicum Actuositatem* 2 and corresponds to *Evangelii Nuntiandi* 73.

Canon 713.3 is dedicated to the clerical Secular Institutes. Preceeding documents state that there are lay as well as clerical Secular Institutes, but no distinct application is mentioned. Now, however, this distinction relative to the apostolate is made in a rather clear way, even though there is a common base of principle in c. 713.1. It can be said that theological reflection is called for on the way specific to priests in assuming the secularity of the Church. The priestly Secular Institutes are now pursuing this reflection.

3. It is also important to recall what the Code says about the <u>form of life</u> in these institutes.

Provida Mater affirmed that they "do not demand life in common" (II and I), yet "they are to have one or more houses in common" for the government, formation, assistance . . . (III and 4).

In practice, initially the Sacred Congregation requested the existence of these houses and extended explicit authorization not to have them. Then the Sacred Congregation no longer requested them and the institutes were free not to have common houses.

The Code does not mention this point and states that the members of Secular Institutes can live on their own, or in their own families, or in small groups of brothers and sisters (c. 714), with the understanding that this latter case is not equivalent to the community life of a typical religious community.

However, no matter what form may be chosen, the Code places very meaningful stress on the fraternal life, the life of brothers and sisters, understood as profound communion in the sense indicated by c. 602.

The communion between the members of the same institute is essential and is brought about in the unity of the same spirit, in the participation in the same charism of consecrated secular life, in the identity of the specific mission, in the fraternity of the reciprocal relationship, and in collaboration in the life of the institute in an active way (c. 716; cf. c. 717.3).

The fraternal life is cultivated through encounters and various types of exchanges: prayer, exchange of experience, dialogue, formation, information, etc.

Conclusion

As pointed out at the beginning, this is not the place for an indepth juridical analysis of the canons. Therefore, a consideration addressed to those called to "assist" a Secular Institue (its groups) as priests: may the Code be for you as well an aid in respecting and enhancing the characteristics of that institute.

APPENDIX A
Part II, Informative Document on Secular Institutes

Sacred Congregation for Religious and Secular Institutes
6 January 1984
(with permission)

Part II—Theological Basis

In the pontifical documents *Provida Mater* and *Primo Feliciter* the theology of Secular Institutes has been dealt with at length, and this has been amplified and investigated fully in Conciliar doctrine and the teaching of the Supreme Pontiffs.

Specialists have also contributed the results of their studies. Yet it must be admitted that the theological research has not by any means ended.

Therefore, what follows is a simple recalling of the main aspects of this theology, referring in substance to the study made by a special Commission and made public with Paul VI's approval in 1976.

1. *The world as "saeculum"*

It was out of love that God created the world, placing man at its centre and summit, and deeming that the created reality was "valde bona," very good (Gen. 1, 31). Man, made through the Word in the image and likeness of God and called upon to live within Christ in the intimate life of God, is given the task of leading all realities, through wisdom and action, to the attainment of this ultimate end. The destiny of the world is therefore bound up with that of man and, consequently, the word "world" is used to designate "the whole human family along with the sum of those realities in midst of which that family lives" (Gaudium et Spes, 2) and in which it works.

The world, therefore, was involved in the initial fall of man and "condemned to lose its purpose" (Rom 8:20), but it is also involved in the redemption brought about by Christ, Saviour of man, Who, through grace, turns him into a son of God and once again capable—by virtue of participation in His Passion and Resurrection—of living and working in the world according to God's plan, for the praise of His glory (cf. Eph. 1:6; 1:12–14).

It is in the light of Revelation, then that the world appears as "saeculum". The "saeculum" is the present world as it results from the initial fall of man, "this world" (1 Cor. 7:31), which subjected to the reign of sin and death, has to come to an end and is placed in antithesis to the "new era" (*aion*), to eternal life inaugurated by the Death and Resurrection of Christ. This world preserves its goodness, truth and essential order, qualities which derive from its condition as something created (cf. GS 36); nevertheless, tarnished by sin as it is, it cannot save itself by its own efforts, but is called upon to share in the salvation brought about by Christ (cf. GS 2, 13, 37, 39), a salvation that is achieved when man—regenerated in faith and baptism, and incorporated in the Church—participates in the Paschal Mystery.

While this salvation is actuated in the course of human history, it penetrates this latter with its light and life; it enlarges and extends its action to all the values of creation, to discern them and to withdraw them from the ambiguity that has characterized them ever since original sin (GS 4), the order to re-establish them in the new freedom of the children of God (cf. Rom 8:21).

2. *New relationship between the baptized and the world*

The Church, a society of persons reborn in Christ to eternal life, is therefore the sacrament of the renewal of the world which will be brought about by the power of the Lord once and for all in the consummation of the "saeculum", accompanied by the destruction of all the powers of the devil, of sin and death, and the subordination of everything to Him and to the Father (cf. 1 Cor. 15:20–28). Through Christ, in the Church, those marked and animated by the Holy Spirit are constituted into a "royal priesthood" (1 Pet 2:9) in which they offer themselves, their activities and their world to the glory of the Father (cfr. Lumen Gentium 34).

For each Christian, therefore, baptism gives rise to a new relationship with and to the world. Together with all other men of good will, the Christian is dedicated to the task of building the world and contributing to the good of humanity, operating in accordance with the legitimate autonomy of terrestrial realities (cfr. GS 34, 36). In fact, this new relationship does not in any way alter or diminish the natural order and, even though it might involve a rupture with the world inasmuch as it is a reality opposed to the life of grace and the expectation of the everlasting kingdom, it also implies the will to work in the love of Christ for the salvation of the world, that is to say, for the leading of humanity to the life of faith and, as far as possible, reordering temporal realities according to God's design, so that they may contribute to man's growth in grace for eternal life (cfr. *Apostolicam Actuositatem* 7).

It is by living this new relationship to the world that the

baptized cooperate in Christ for the world's redemption. Consequently, the "secularity" of a baptized person—here seen as existence in this world and participation in its manifold activities—can never be understood outside the framework of this essential relationship, whatever concrete form it may assume.

3. *Diversity in concretely living the relationship to the world*

All must live this essential relationship to the world and tend towards that sanctity that is participation in the divine life, in charity. (cfr. LG 40). But there remains the fact that God distributes his gifts to each of us "in proportion to what Christ has given" (Eph 4:7).

In fact, God is sovereignly free in the distribution of his gifts. In his free initiative, the Spirit of God distributes them: "As he wishes he gives a different gift to each person" (1 Cor 12:11), having in mind not only the good of the individual person but, at one and the same time, also the global interest of the entire Church and the whole of mankind.

It is in very virtue of this wealth of gifts that the fundamental unity of the Mystical Body that is the Church manifests itself in the complementary diversities of its members, who live and work under the action of the Spirit of Christ for the building up of his Body.

In fact, the universal vocation to sanctity in the Church is cultivated in the various kinds of life and in the various functions (cfr. LG 41) according to the manifold specific vocations. The Lord accompanies these different vocations with the gifts needed to enable a person to live them. Furthermore, these vocations, encountering the free response of the persons concerned, give rise to different ways of realization. Consequently, there will also be differences in the ways in which Christians give concrete form to their baptismal relationship to the world.

4. *Following Christ in the practice of the Evangelical Counsels*

Following Christ signifies for every Christian an absolute preference for Him, if necessary to the point of martyrdom (cfr. LG 42). But Christ invites some of his faithful to follow him unconditionally in order to dedicate themselves totally to Him and to the coming of the Kingdom of Heaven. This is a call to an irrevocable act that implies a complete donation of oneself to the person of Christ to share his life, his mission, his destiny, and, as a condition, the renunciation of one's own self, of married life and of material goods.

This renunciation is lived by those called as a condition that enables them to adhere without hindrance to that absolute Love which centres them in Christ and thus permits them to enter more intimately into the movement of this Love towards creation: "God loved the world so much that he gave his only son" (Jn 3:16) so that, through him, the world might be saved. Such a decision, by virtue of its total and definitive response to the exigencies of love, assumes the character of a vow of absolute fidelity to Christ. It clearly presupposes the baptismal premise of living as a faithful follower of Christ, but is distinguished from it, perfecting it.

By virtue of its content, this decision radicalizes the relationship of the baptized to the world, because one's renunciation of "using this world" in the usual manner bears witness to its relative and provisional value and foretells the coming of the eschatological kingdom (cfr. 1 Cor. 8:31).

In the Church the content of this donation has assumed the form of the practice of the "evangelical counsels" (consecrated chastity, poverty, obedience) concretely lived in different ways, spontaneous or institutionalized. The diversity of these forms is due to the different ways in which one can work with Christ for the salvation of the world, ways that may range from the effective separation that is peculiar to certain forms of religious life right through to the presence typical to the members of Secular Institutes.

The presence of these latter in the midst of the world signifies a special vocation to a salvific presence that expresses itself in bearing witness to Christ and in an activity that aims at ordering temporal realities according to God's plan. In relation to this activity the profession of the evangelical counsels assumes the special significance of liberation from the obstacles (pride, cupidity) that prevent one from seeing and putting into practice the order desired by God.

5. *Ecclesiality of the Profession of the Evangelical Counsels— Consecration*

Every call to follow Christ is a call to a communion of life in Him and in the Church.

Consequently, the practice and profession of the evangelical counsels in the Church have expressed themselves not only in an individual manner, but also by insertion into communities brought into being by the Holy Spirit through the charism of their founders.

These communities are intimately linked with the life of the Church animated by the Holy Spirit and therefore entrusted to the discernment and the judgement of the hierarchy that is called to verify their charisms, to admit them, to approve them and to send them on their way, recognizing their mission of cooperating in the building up of the kingdom of God.

The total and definitive donation to Christ undertaken by the members of these Institutes is therefore received, in the name of the Church—as the representative of Christ—and in the form approved by her, by the constituted authorities within these institutes, so as to create a sacred bond (cfr. LG 44). In fact, by accepting the donation of a person, the Church marks that person in the name of God with a special consecration as belonging exclusively to Christ and to his work of salvation.

The sacramental and fundamental consecration of man is constituted by baptism, but this consecration can then be lived in a more or less "profound and intimate" manner. The firm decision to answer the special call of Christ, totally and freely donating to him one's whole existence and forsaking everything in the world that can create an obstacle or impediment to such an exclusive donation, offers material for the so-called new consecration (cfr. LG 44) which is "deeply rooted in their baptismal consecration, and provides an ampler manifestation of it" (*Perfectae Caritatis* 5). It is the action of God that calls the person, whom he reserves for himself through the ministry of the Church, and whom he assists with special graces to enable him or her to remain faithful.

The Consecration of the members of Secular Institutes is not marked by a setting aside, made visible by external signs but it nevertheless possesses the essential characteristic of a total dedication to Christ in a specific ecclesial community; community with which the member contracts a reciprocal and stable bond and in the charism of which he participates. From this there follows a particular consequence regarding the manner in which one must understand obedience in Secular Institutes: it involves not only a search—either individually or in group—for God's will in assuming those duties proper to a secular life, but also the free acceptance of the mediation of the Church and the community through its authorities within the limits of the constitutive Norms of the individual institutes.

6. *The "secularity" of Secular Institutes*

The *following of Christ* in the practice of the evangelical counsels has had the effect of creating within the Church a state of life characterized by a certain "abandonment of the 'saeculum'": religious life. This state has therefore come to be distinguished from that of the faithful remaining in the conditions and activities of the world, faithful who are therefore referred to as *"seculars"*.

Thus, having recognized new institutes in which the evangelical counsels are fully professed by faithful who remain in the world and are committed to its activities, working for its salvation from within ("in saeculo ac veluti ex saeculo"), the Church has therefore called these institutes *"Secular Institutes"*.

In the quality of *secular* attributed to these Institutes there is what might be called a "negative" meaning: they are not religious (cfr. PC 11), so that legislation or proceedings proper to religious should not be applied to them.

But the really important meaning that brings out their specific vocation is *"positive"*: secularity indicates either a sociological condition—of being in the world—, or an attitude of apostolic commitment that takes into account the values of temporal realities and acts from them, in order to impregnate them with an evangelical spirit.

The commitment is lived in a different manner by lay persons and priests. The former, in fact, have a particular note that characterizes their very evangelization and their witness to the faith in words and works, namely "to search for the kingdom of God by dealing with temporal realities and re-ordering them according to God." (LG 31). Priests, on the other hand, except in unusual cases (cfr. LG 31, PO 8)—do not exercise this responsibility towards the world by means of direct and immediate action in the temporal order, but rather through their ministerial action and by means of their role as educators in the faith (cfr. Presbyterorum Ordinis 6): this is the supreme means for making contribution towards ensuring that the world will continuously perfect itself in accordance with the order and the significance of creation (Paul VI, February 2, 1972), and for giving the laity "the moral and spiritual aids by which the temporal order can be restored in Christ" (AA 7).

Though by virtue of their consecration, Secular Institutes are included among institutes of consecrated life, the characteristic of secularity distinguishes them from all other forms of institutes.

The merging in one and the same vocation of consecration and secular commitment confers an original note upon both these elements. The full profession of the evangelical counsels ensures that a more intimate union with Christ will make the apostolate in the world particularly fruitful. The secular commitment confers a special modality upon the very profession of the evangelical counsels and stimulates this profession towards an ever greater evangelical authenticity.

APPENDIX B
Canons 710-730
Code of Canon Law

Title III
Secular Institutes

Can. 710—A secular institute is an institute of consecrated life in which the Christian faithful living in the world strive for the perfection of charity and work for the sanctification of the world especially from within.

Can. 711—The consecration of a member of a secular institute does not alter the member's proper canonical condition among the people of God, whether lay or clerical, with due regard for the prescriptions of law affecting institutes of consecrated life.

Can. 712—With due regard for the prescriptions of cann. 598–601, the constitutions are to determine the sacred bonds by which the evangelical counsels are taken in the institute and are to define the obligations flowing from these same bonds, while always preserving, however, in its way of life the distinctive secularity of the institute.

Can. 713—§1. The members of these institutes express and exercise their own consecration in their apostolic activity and like a leaven they strive to imbue all things with the spirit of the gospel for the strengthening and growth of the Body of Christ.

§2. Lay members share in the Church's evangelizing task in the world and of the world through their witness of a Christian life and fidelity toward their consecration, and through their efforts to order temporal things according to God and inform the world by the power of the gospel. Also, they cooperate in serving the ecclesial community, according to their particular secular way of life.

§3. Clerical members through the witness of their consecrated life, especially in the presbyterate, help their brothers by their special apostolic charity and in their sacred ministry among the people of God they bring about the sanctification of the world.

Can. 714—Members are to lead their life according to the norm of the constitutions, in the ordinary conditions of the world, either alone or each in their respective families, or in a group of brothers or sisters.

Can. 715—§1. Clerical members incardinated in a diocese depend on the diocesan bishop, with due regard for those things which pertain to consecrated life in their particular institute.

§2. If those who are incardinated in an institute according to the norm of can. 266, §3, are appointed to particular works of the institute or to the governance of the institute, they depend on the bishop in a way comparable to religious.

Can. 716—§1. All members are to share actively in the life of the institute according to proper law.

§2. Members of the same institute are to maintain communion among themselves, carefully fostering unity of spirit and genuine relationship as brothers or sisters.

Can. 717—§1. The constitutions are to prescribe a particular manner of governance and define the time during which moderators hold their office and the way in which they are chosen.

§2. No one is to be chosen supreme moderator who is not definitively incorporated.

§3. Those who are put in charge of the governance of the institute are to take care that the unity of its spirit is kept and that active participation of the members is encouraged.

Can. 718—The administration of the goods of the institute, which should express and foster evangelical poverty, is ruled by the norms of Book V, *The Temporal Goods of the Church,* and by the proper law of the institute. Likewise the proper law is to define especially the financial obligations of the institute toward members who carry on work for it.

Can. 719—§1. In order that members may respond faithfully to their vocation and that their apostolic action may proceed from their union with Christ they are to be diligent in prayer, concentrate in a fitting manner on the reading of Sacred Scripture, make an annual retreat and carry out other spiritual exercises according to proper law.

§2. The celebration of the Eucharist, daily if possible, is to be the source and strength of the whole of their consecrated life.

§3. They are freely to approach the sacrament of penance, which they should receive frequently.

§4. They are freely to obtain necessary guidance of conscience and should seek counsel of this kind even from their moderators, if they wish.

Can. 720—The right of admission into the institute, whether for probation or for the assumption of sacred bonds, whether temporary or perpetual or definitive, pertains to the major moderators with their council according to the norm of the constitutions.

Can. 721—§1. One is invalidly admitted to the initial probation:

1° who has not yet reached the age of majority;

2° who is still bound by a sacred bond in some institute of consecrated life or who is incorporated in a society of apostolic life;

3° who is married while the marriage lasts.

§2. The constitutions can establish other impediments, even for the validity of admission, or place certain conditions.

§3. Moreover, for one to be received it is necessary to have the maturity to lead the life proper to the institute.

Can. 722—§1. The initial probation is to be so arranged that the candidates may understand more fittingly their divine vocation and indeed the vocation proper to the institute and may be trained in the spirit and way of life of the institute.

§2. The candidates are to be properly formed in living according to the evangelical counsels and taught to translate this life completely into the apostolate, using those forms of spreading the gospel which better respond to the purpose, spirit and character of the institute.

§3. The manner and time of this probation before first undertaking sacred bonds in the institute are to be defined in the constitutions; yet it is to be no less than two years.

Can. 723—§1. After the time of the initial probation has passed, the candidate who is judged worthy is either to take on the three evangelical counsels strengthened by a sacred bond or to depart from the institute.

§2. This first incorporation, no shorter than five years, is to be temporary according to the norm of the constitutions.

§3. When the time of this incorporation has passed, the member who is judged worthy is to be admitted to perpetual or definitive incorporation, that is, with temporary bonds always to be renewed.

§4. Definitive incorporation is equivalent to perpetual incorporation as far as certain juridic effects are concerned, to be determined in the constitutions.

Can. 724—§1. After the sacred bonds are first taken formation is to be continued according to the constitutions.

§2. Members are to be formed in divine and human matters equally; the moderators of the institute are to take seriously the continuing spiritual formation of members.

Can. 725—The institute can associate to itself, by some bond determined in the constitutions, other members of the Christian faithful who strive toward evangelical perfection according to the spirit of the institute and share its mission.

Can. 726—§1. When the time of temporary incorporation has elapsed, the member can leave the institute freely or be excluded from renewal of the sacred bonds for a just cause by the major moderator after hearing the council.

§2. For a serious reason the temporarily incorporated member can freely petition and obtain from the supreme moderator with the consent of the council an indult to leave.

Can. 727—§1. The perpetually incorporated member who wishes to leave the institute, having thought seriously about this before God, may seek an indult to leave from the Apostolic See through the supreme moderator if it is an institute of pontifical right; otherwise from the diocesan bishop as it is defined in the constitutions.

§2. If it is a question of a cleric incardinated in the institute, the prescription of can. 693 is to be observed.

Can. 728—When the indult to leave has been legitimately granted, all bonds, rights and obligations emanating from incorporation cease.

Can. 729—A member is dismissed from the institute according to the norm established in cann. 694 and 695; furthermore, the constitutions may determine other causes of dismissal, provided they are proportionately serious, external, imputable, and juridically proven and the procedure determined in cann. 697–700 shall be observed. The prescription of can. 701 applies to the dismissed member.

Can. 730—In order that a member of a secular institute may transfer to another secular institute, the prescriptions of cann. 684, §§1,2, and 4 and 685 are to be observed. In order that a transfer be made to a religious institute or to a society of apostolic life or from these to a secular institute, the permission of the Apostolic See is required and its mandates are to be obeyed.

Bibliography

Acts of the International Congress of Secular Institutes. Rome. September 1970.

Albertini, Mario. "Authority in Secular Institutes." *Consecrated Life.* 1987. pp 63–68.

Asian Conference of Secular Institutes. Poona, Bangkok: National Vocation Service Centre, Dept. of Secular Institutes. 1975.

At the Heart of History: Acts of the Second International Congress of Secular Institutes. Rome: World Conference of Secular Institutes. August 1980.

Beyer, Jean. *Religious Life or Secular Institute.* Rome: Gregorian University Press. 1970.

Dialogue. International Journal of Secular Institutes. Rome: World Conference of Secular Institutes.

Holland, Sr. Sharon, I.H.M. "The Concept of Consecration in Secular Institutes." Diss. Rome. 1981.

Malloy, Thomas E. "Secular Institutes." In *A Handbook on Canons 573-746.* Ed. Hite, et al. Collegeville, MN: The Liturgical Press. 1985. pp 278–279.

Memoria in Secolarita e Vita Consecrata. Ed. A. Oberti. Milano. 1966.

O'Connor, David F. "Two Forms of Consecrated Life: Religious and Secular Institutes." *Review for Religious.* Vol 46, 1986. pp 205–19.

Olmsted, Thomas J. "The Secularity of Secular Institutes." Diss. Rome: Pontifical Gregorian Institute. 1981.

Reedy, Gabriel, O.F.M. *Secular Institutes.* New York: Hawthorne Books. 1962.

Secular Prayer: Acts of the Second International Assembly. Rome: World Conference of Secular Institutes. 1976.

Way Supplement on Secular Institutes. No. 12, Spring 1971.

Additional Resources

Benedict XVI. "To the Participants on the International Symposium of Secular Institutes." *Dialogue.* Vol. XXXV, 2007, No. 152-153, pp. 27-31

George Card. Cottier, OP, "Theological Aspects of Secular Consecration." *Dialogue.* Vol XXXV, 2007, No. 152-153, pp. 14-25.

John Paul II. Apostolic Exhortation, *Christifideles Laici. (Lay members of Christ's Faithful People.)* December 30, 1998.

John Paul II. Apostolic Exhortation, *Vita Consecrata. (Consecrated Life.)* March 25, 1996.

John Paul II. *The Private Prayers of Pope John Paul II.* New York, NY: Pocket Books, Copyright 1994 Libreria Editrice Rogate.

Secular Institutes: Their Identity And Their Mission. Rome: World Congress of Secular Institutes, May 1983.

Sharon Holland, IHM. "Make Christ the Heart of the World' A Canonical Reflection On Secular Institutes." *Dialogue.* Vol. XXXV, 2007, No 152-153, pp. 44-57

Notes